The Son of Prophecy

The Son of Prophecy

Henry Tudor's
Road to Bosworth

David Rees

JOHN JONES

For Richard

The Son of Prophecy: Henry Tudor's Road to Bosworth

© David Rees 1997

First published by Black Raven Press, 1985

Second, revised, edition published by John Jones Publishing Ltd, October 1997

ISBN 1 871083 01 X

Cover design by Ruth Evans, Welsh Books Council

Printed in Wales by CIT Printing Services, Haverfordwest

Principal distributors: The Welsh Books Council Distribution Centre, Llanbadarn, Aberystwyth.

Published by JOHN JONES PUBLISHING LTD., Registered Office, Barclays Bank Chambers, St. Peter's Square, Ruthin, Denbighshire.

Contents

Illustrations

Plates

Maps

Genealogical Tables

Acknowledgements

I should like to express my thanks to the Librarian of the London Library and the staff of the National Library of Wales for their help during the writing of this book. I also wish to thank Reginald and Marjorie Piggott for their assistance during the preparation of the maps.

I owe a special dept of gratitude to the works of Professor Glanmor Williams, Major Francis Jones and Professor Ralph A. Griffiths whose writings are, of course, indispensable to any student of the period covered in this book.

The map of the Battle of Bosworth is based on a map in *The Battle of Bosworth* by D. T. Williams, first published by the Leicester University Press in association with the Corporation of Leicester.

The permission of the following to reproduce illustrations is gratefully acknowledged:

Mr. Douglas Hardy for Plate 1(a); the former Dyfed Cultural Services Department for Plate 1(b); the Master and Fellows, St John's College, Cambridge for Plate 2(a); the Dean and Chapter of Westminster Abbey for Plate 2(b); Mrs. Olive Smith for the photographs by Edwin Smith reproduced as Plates 3 and 4.

The map of the Battle of Bosworth Field is based on a map in *The Battle of Bosworth* by D. T. Williams, first published by Leicester University Press in association with the Corporation of Leicester.

The Son of Prophecy: Preface

It has often been observed that Henry Tudor was an improbable pretender to the English Crown in 1485. Such hereditary claim as he had came through his mother, whose own status in the succession was a matter of dispute. The alleged prediction by Henry VI that the son of his half brother Edmund Tudor would one day succeed him, is based upon no contemporary evidence and was almost certainly invented during Henry's reign. His close connection with the Lancastrian royal house, which carried no rights to the Crown, derived from the marriage of Henry V's widow, Catherine de Valois, to the Welsh squire Owen Tudor. It was this connection which caused their son Edmund to be raised to the Earldom of Richmond, the title which Henry held before his deprivation in 1462, and which he continued to claim.

In spite of his name, Henry was only 25% Welsh by blood, two of his grandparents being English, and one French. He lived in Wales as a young child, and must have learned some of his early speech from his Welsh nurse. However, he grew up and received his education mainly in Brittany. As an adult he was equally fluent in English and French, and had a modest grasp of ecclesiastical Latin, but there is no evidence that he either spoke or understood Welsh.

In spite of this, his sense of Welsh identity, and the personal loyalty of the Welsh to him, both remained strong. This was partly because the influential bards had identified him as *mab darogan*, the 'son of prophecy'. The prophecy in question was one attributed to Merlin, which claimed that a Welsh prince would one day conquer England and restore the ancient Celtic hegemony. Henry was not the first to be so identified, but he was the first whose achievement approximated to expectation. As king he was not one to turn his back upon loyal service, however it arose, and since he actually did very little for his Welsh subjects, occasional demonstrations of Welsh sympathy were useful to keep that loyalty alive.

The study which follows is not only an investigation into how Henry put together the resources to support his bid, but also how the ancient prophecy disposed the Welsh to support him when few others could see the merits in his cause. It constitutes a salutary reminder that there is more to politics than a calculation of interests. Continuing interest in this important subject has prompted John Jones to reissue the work in this format, with an updated bibliography.

David Loades
Emeritus Professor of History,
University of Wales

Introduction

On 1 August 1485 a small fleet of ships left the Norman port of Harfleur for Wales. The leader of the expedition, Henry Tudor, Earl of Richmond, had for the past fourteen years lived in exile in Brittany and France. Most of the 2,000 men who accompanied him were French soldiers – not of the first quality – who had been provided by the King of France. There were also some English and Welsh supporters of Henry, including his uncle, Jasper Tudor, Earl of Pembroke. It was a slender force with which to win its objective, the throne of England.

Henry Tudor's expedition was expected by Richard III. Following the collapse of Buckingham's revolt in late 1483, the English king, a veteran soldier and administrator, had organized a series of measures to counter the expected landing. Troops had been mustered, beacons prepared and castles garrisoned. In west Wales, where Henry was to land, the castles of Tenby, Pembroke, Manorbier, Haverfordwest and Cilgerran, the gateway to Cardiganshire, had been put in a state of readiness. Moreover, a man loyal to Richard III, William Herbert, Earl of Huntingdon, was justice of south Wales, which gave him authority over the royal counties of Carmarthen and Cardigan. Herbert was also in control of Brecon and other castles in the Welsh Marches.

Richard himself had taken up position at Nottingham Castle in the summer of 1485, a central strategic point from which to move quickly against any landing in his realm. In a proclamation in June 1485, the King called on his 'natural and true' subjects to defend themselves against the invader. According to the Tudor chronicler, Edward Hall, Richard regarded his adversary as 'an unknown Welshman, whose father I never knew, nor him personally met . . .'

But Richard III's position was not as strong as it seemed. In April 1484 his only son and heir apparent died. Less than a year later in March 1485 his wife, Queen Anne, also died. The future of the dynasty

1

was thus in question, and this uncertainty was compounded by the growing conviction in the kingdom that Richard was responsible for the murder of his nephews, sons of Edward IV, in the Tower during the summer of 1483.

There was also a widespread political conspiracy against Richard III in which a central role was probably played by Henry Tudor's mother, Lady Margaret Beaufort. She was married to Thomas, Lord Stanley, head of the powerful Stanley clan influential in north Wales, Cheshire and the borders.

Strong national sentiment generally existed in Wales in favour of Henry Tudor, with his family links to Anglesey and with the old ruling families of north and west Wales. Jasper Tudor, moreover, had been active in the Lancastrian cause in Wales for thirty years. These factors pointed towards Wales as the focus of Henry Tudor's expedition. In a letter to one of his supporters in Wales, John ap Meredith, Henry Tudor had already claimed that the crown was rightfully his, expressed his confidence in 'the nobles and commons of this our principality of Wales', and promised to deliver the Welsh people 'of such miserable servitudes as they piteously long stood in'.

In calm weather, Henry Tudor and his men landed at Mill Bay, the first cove inside the north side of Milford Haven, on the evening of Sunday, 7 August 1485. That same evening Henry's forces advanced to the village of Dale, two miles to the north. The following morning, 8 August, they began their march north through Haverfordwest and along the Cardiganshire coast to Shrewsbury. Two weeks later, on 22 August, against odds that still seem considerable, Richard III was killed at Bosworth Field and Henry Tudor was acclaimed as King Henry on the battlefield. The Tudor era had begun.

> On a bare Leicestershire upland [wrote G. M. Trevelyan] a few thousand men in close conflict foot to foot, while a few thousand more stood aside to watch the issue, sufficed to set upon the throne of England the greatest of all her royal lines, that should guide her through a century of change down new and larger streams of destiny, undreamt of by any men who plied bow and bill on that day in the old-world quarrel of York and Lancaster. . .[1]

It was Henry's ambition to link and to reconcile York and Lancaster not only with his marriage to Elizabeth of York, Edward IV's daughter, in 1486, but also in the symbolism of the Tudor 'Double Rose' which he probably invented. During the civil wars of the fifteenth century, there was no Red Rose of Lancaster, and an often-employed Lancastrian badge was the White Swan of Bohun which Henry V had taken from his mother. The White Rose was only one device used by the Yorkists, who also displayed the Falcon and Fetterlock and Edward IV's Sun in Splendour. Richard III's personal badge was the White Boar. But Henry VII's adoption of the Red Rose, and his use of the fused Red and White Rose to symbolize his role as the unifier of Lancaster and York, quickly gained popularity. The so-called 'Tudor myth' passed to historians of the reign, and the chroniclers of the sixteenth century hailed Bosworth as an event which ended a century of internecine conflict. This view remains immortalized by Shakespeare's genius in Richmond's speech at the close of *Richard III*:

> We will unite the white rose and the red;
> Smile heaven upon this fair conjunction
> That hath long frown'd upon their enmity!
> What traitor hears me, and says not amen?
> England hath long been mad, and scarr'd herself . . .
> O! now, let Richmond and Elizabeth,
> The true succeeders of each royal house,
> By God's fair ordinance conjoin together;
> And let their heirs – God, if thy will be so –
> Enrich the time to come with smooth'd-fac'd peace,
> With smiling plenty, and fair prosperous days!

But the significance of Bosworth Field, as it has passed down the centuries, has transcended even the union of the Red Rose and the White. The battle is usually viewed as the beginning of far-reaching developments in politics, the nature of the monarchy and religion that transformed England and later Great Britain. We still tend to think of 1485 as a year which separates the feudal from the modern era, a demarcation between profoundly different ways of looking at society.

Moreover, whatever the precise historical significance of the Tudor accession, there can be no doubt of the enduring importance of 1485 in English dynastic history.

Ever since Bosworth, the crown has remained vested in the descendants of Henry VII. The direct line of the Tudors came to an end with the death of Elizabeth, Henry Tudor's grand-daughter. But from the marriage of Henry's daughter, Margaret, to James IV of Scotland stemmed the union of the crowns under the Stuarts. Although the direct, or stictly legitimist, descent was modified by Parliament in 1689 and in 1701 to allow for the Protestant succession, the victor of Bosworth Field founded a dynastic system that has now lasted half a millennium.

All this rich historical tapestry stems from Henry Tudor's victory at Bosworth in 1485. But what was the Welsh contribution to the victory, bearing in mind that in Wales Henry was welcomed as a long-expected national saviour? Henry's victory, it should be recalled, was won by an army initially outnumbered. By all the odds, the day should have been won by Richard III.

But apathy and calculated defection – or treachery – by forces formally loyal to Richard III was decisive. One of Richard's senior commanders, Northumberland, made no move on the field of battle, and the forces of the Stanleys waited for the opportune moment to move decisively against Richard III and despatch the last Plantagenet as in a final desperate charge he came near to killing Henry Tudor. Thomas, Lord Stanley then crowned the victor with Richard III's crown or coronet which had been found amongst the debris of the battle.

Henry Tudor's entire strategy which culminated at Bosworth was contingent on his unopposed march through Wales to the heart of England. On the road from Dale to Shrewsbury, a distance of about 150 miles covered in six days, Henry faced the potential obstacles of great castles and a difficult terrain, obstacles which in the past had proved formidable barriers to both kings of England and Welsh princes. Henry VII's latest and perhaps most authoritative biographer, S. B. Chrimes, has written that 'he owed much, perhaps everything in his final progress towards Bosworth to either Welsh support or at least Welsh abstention from opposition in the crucial days of August 1485'.[2]

No contemporary account of Bosworth survives, but Polydore Vergil, writing over twenty years after the battle, recorded that Rhys ap Thomas brought 'a great bande of soldiers' to Henry's support. This force moved eastwards along the Tywi valley and northwards from Brecon through central Wales to a prearranged meeting with Henry

Tudor at Long Mountain (Cefn Digoll) near Welshpool on 13 August 1485. Other contingents from north Wales joined Henry at the same time. The next day the gates of Shrewsbury were closed against the invaders, but on 15 August 1485 the town welcomed Henry's forces. The most difficult part of the march to Bosworth was over.

The unopposed march through Wales, when resistance could have meant disaster, was thus a prerequisite for victory at Bosworth. There had been a thorough preparation, and bardic prophecies, drawing on a long poetic tradition, were central to Henry Tudor's acceptance as a Son of Prophecy (*Mab Darogan*), or national deliverer, who would rule in London. No doubt some in this bardic class hoped that Henry Tudor would establish Welsh supremacy over the English, for this was the logical outcome of the ancient prophecies. But these hopes were unrealistic, as Henry Tudor sought to win, and keep, the English crown. Revenge over the Saxons, or the sons of Rowena, was irrelevant.

Rather more realistic in their support of Henry Tudor were those leaders of the Welsh gentry who rallied to him in 1485. To these natural leaders of society, who had emerged out of the ruins of tribalism in the previous two centuries, the appeal of national sentiment was a powerful one.

But the Welsh gentry also expected lasting political and economic advantages from Henry's success such as the full privileges of Englishmen, which were denied them, at least formally, by penal legislation dating back to the rebellion of Owain Glyn Dŵr (Owen Glendower) and earlier. The aim of this gentry class was not the national independence that Glyn Dŵr had fought for, but rather the discovery of an effective long-term champion of their political interests within the English political system. Sentiment, realism and self-interest alike thus indicated support of Henry Tudor in 1485. The hopes and interests of the gentry were more practical, more personal, than those of the bards, for survival in the pitiless world of fifteenth-century politics dictated strict avoidance of lost causes and lost leaders.

The first Tudor, with his Welsh roots, no doubt recognized these disparate forces which brought him indispensable support in Wales. He promised to right ancient wrongs in Wales, but in the wider context of English politics he claimed the throne as the heir of Lancaster through his mother, Lady Margaret Beaufort, who was descended from John of Gaunt, third son of Edward III. Although regarded as tenuous by some, this was the essence of his claim, made absolute by the divine judgment which, it was asserted, gave him victory at Bosworth.

But Henry also claimed an older legitimacy by virtue of his descent from the early Welsh rulers of Britain through his father, Edmund Tudor, Earl of Richmond. He marched through Wales in 1485 under the Red Dragon standard of Cadwaladr, which after Bosworth was presented at St Paul's. Along with the greyhound of Richmond, the symbolism of the Welsh dragon on his coinage, as the dexter supporter of his royal arms, and finally chiselled in the stone above his tomb in Westminster Abbey, tells its own story.

Moreover, Henry Tudor's victory in 1485 brought both a pyschological union of England and Wales, later ratified in Henry VIII's legislation, and a new era of peace, prosperity and confidence to his Welsh gentry supporters. These squires, who needed little prompting, were finally persuaded by Bosworth Field that they and their new dynasty were the rightful sons of the old Trojan rulers of Britain, in line with the influential prophecies of Geoffrey of Monmouth.[3]

To understand the forces that brought this initially improbable Son of Prophecy through Wales to Bosworth Field, the English crown and immortality, we must begin with the great rebellion of Owain Glyn Dŵr. It was this historic uprising that began the story that ended at Bosworth Field.

1

The Great Rebellion

On 11 December 1282 the last native Prince of Wales, Llewellyn ap Gruffydd of Gwynedd, met his death in a skirmish at Cilmeri, near Builth. The following year his brother David was taken and executed at Shrewsbury. The death of these princes terminated a dynasty that had ruled in Wales since the departure of the Romans. It was the end of Welsh independence, and the bitter laments of the bards ring down the centuries.

Yet the Welsh identity was not extinguished, and successive hopes for a national revival during the next two centuries provide the historical key for understanding the welcome given to Henry Tudor in 1485. Moreover, events between 1282 and 1485 do much to explain the policies which affect life in Wales to the present day.

In the first aftermath of the defeat of 1282, it was difficult to see how Welsh national hopes could ever be fulfilled. Events in the two generations leading up to the death of Llewellyn the Last had sombre implications as English castles and boroughs spread across Wales.

Between the Anglo-Saxon invasions and the Norman conquest of England in 1066, Wales had preserved its independence, but despite a common language, literature and legal system, the country was divided into a number of small kingdoms, often in conflict with each other as well as with the English. Anglo-Saxon England, on the other hand, had become a unified state by the time of the coming of the Normans. Prior to 1066, however, the geography of Wales, with its rugged terrain and its isolation, had preserved it from British conquest. A border had evolved between English and Welsh rulers based approximately on the demarcation line of Offa's Dyke.

This political relationship changed quickly after the Norman conquest of England under King William. Taking advantage of internecine rivalries amongst the Welsh, and deploying modern military techniques that had brought them victories elsewhere in Europe, Norman barons advanced along the northern and southern coastal plains of Wales. The Normans also advanced westwards along the historic river routes that lead into Wales from Shrewsbury and Hereford. In eastern and southern Wales especially, a network of Norman lordships, their borders often following those of the Welsh commotes they supplanted, had been established by the year 1200. The March, or Marches, of Wales had come into existence.

These Norman Marcher lords claimed the regal, independent powers of the rulers they displaced, and owed only titular homage to the English king. Norman rulers quickly built a system of castles, at first of wood, then of stone, to dominate their lordships. A line of castles soon ran along the Welsh border from north to south, and across south and west Wales from the Severn to the Irish Sea. It was now that Chepstow, Newport and Cardiff, Swansea and Brecon, Pembroke, Haverfordwest and Cardigan came into existence. In the shadow of the Norman castle there usually stood an Anglo-Norman borough. Marcher lordships were often divided into a low-lying Englishry and an upland Welshry where native tribal law and pastoral farming continued.

Throughout the twelfth and most of the thirteenth centuries, the three leading Welsh principalities resisted Norman penetration. But social and cultural links with England developed in the general context of medieval civilization. There was a considerable amount of intermarriage between the leading Welsh and Norman families.

In the north, Llewellyn the Great (d. 1240) and Llewellyn the Last (d. 1282) of Gwynedd tried to create a feudalized Welsh state to counter the Norman advance. In central Wales the weaker princes of Powys ruled over the Severn valley and the mountains to the north-east. To the south, the princes of Deheubarth, governing from the ancient royal castle of Dinefwr (Dynevor), and territorially based in Carmarthenshire and Cardiganshire, succeeded in limiting Norman expansion under the tough policies of the Lord Rhys (d. 1197).

The Statute of Rhuddlan

Despite the determination of the two Llewellyns, who increasingly took the lead in the Welsh cause during the thirteenth century, the political and strategic odds were against the Welsh. Although King Henry III (d. 1272) recognized Llewellyn ap Gruffydd as Prince of Wales in 1267 with the Treaty of Montgomery, Henry's son, Edward I (d. 1307), one of the outstanding English medieval monarchs, proved too much of a match for the ambitions of the last Llewellyn. The death of that prince in 1282 thus effectively ended Welsh independence. The territories of Gwynedd in north Wales now became crown possessions, as did the lands of the heirs of the Lord Rhys in south-west Wales.

After the Conquest of 1282–3, Edward I instituted a historic programme of castle building to guard against a Welsh resurgence. A dozen new castles were built, half a dozen others were reconstructed, and adjacent to these fortresses new boroughs planted with loyal English officials and traders soon sprang into existence. Some of the boroughs were built as walled towns as a further security measure.

There was an organic relationship between castle and borough in that the new towns helped to solve the logistic problems of supplying castles in potentially hostile country. The great Edwardian castles of Conwy, Caernarfon and Harlech, some of the most impressive fortresses in the world, still stand as a historic reminder of the military side of the Edwardian settlement in Wales. But perhaps of even greater significance was the interrelated Edwardian political and administrative settlement in Wales.

Under King Edward's Statute of Rhuddlan (1284), the former lands of Gwynedd became the royal counties of Caernarfon, Merioneth and Anglesey. The separate county of Flint was placed under the King's justice of Chester. In the south, the Statute of Rhuddlan recognized the two royal counties of Carmarthen and Cardigan, mostly lands which, as we have seen, had formerly belonged to the last lords of Deheubarth. Only Rhys ap Maredudd of Dryslwyn retained his patrimony, while legally subordinate to royal officials in Carmarthen Castle. But with his fatal revolt in 1287, his lands too became crown territory.

Edward I also introduced the machinery of English local government into these royal possessions in Wales which after 1301 were vested in the king's eldest son as Prince of Wales and were thus now known as the Principality. The new institutions of administration included shires and hundreds, sheriffs and coroners. The Principality was of course quite separate from the March of Wales, and was also constitutionally (and geographically) distinct from the realm of England.

Furthermore, these royal counties in Wales were organized into two groups in north and south Wales ruled from Caernarfon and Carmarthen Castles respectively. The royal administration in each group was headed by a justiciar (or justice) and a chamberlain. The justiciar held supreme executive and judicial powers, analogous to a viceroy, while the chamberlain headed the exchequer. In practice much of the work of these two high officials was carried out by deputies. Later convenience dictated that these two parts of the royal administration became known as the 'Principality of north Wales' and the 'Principality of south Wales'.

As the Principality was separate from the March, which was further subdivided into scores of Marcher lordships, there were thus two broad forms of government in Wales from 1284 to 1536, when the entire system was swept away by Henry VIII. It was the shortcomings inherent in this system, combined with the restrictions of local English officialdom, that led first to Welsh support for Owain Glyn Dŵr and then for Henry Tudor.

The Edwardian Settlement

At first, the Edwardian settlement in Wales seemed to work reasonably well. Although the key, higher positions in the royal administration were occupied by Englishmen, local government on the hundred or commote level was invariably the preserve of Welshmen, usually drawn from the ranks of the *uchelwyr*, or gentlemen. It has been noted that of the forty-four sheriffs who served in the three new north Welsh counties between 1284 and 1343, eleven seem to have been Welsh. Non-residence of justices and sheriffs provided further opportunities for Welshmen to become their deputies.

Although English criminal and common law was brought into the royal courts of the Principality, Welsh civil law was not abolished. In any case, those Welshmen who were already building landed estates found the English law of property more convenient to their purposes. The Welsh custom of gavelkind, or partible inheritance, led to the subdivision of family land. So the English law of primogeniture was naturally preferred in some circumstances. In the March, an amalgam of English law, Welsh law and local custom prevailed, differing from lordship to lordship, and generally known as 'the Law of the March'. Here in the March, even more than in the Principality, the holding of office by Welshmen was a central factor in the growth of an official class of gentry families.

Two of the leaders of this official class of Welshmen in the early fourteenth century were Sir Gruffydd Llwyd in north Wales and Sir Rhys ap Gruffydd in south Wales. But other, less prominent Welshmen enlisted in the English armies which fought in France and Scotland. Welsh archers, for example, deploying their lethal longbows, were prominent at Crécy (1346) and Poitiers (1356).

The Red Dragon of Cadwaladr was already recognized as the flag of these contingents who fought for the English crown. Overall, it may well have been that the creation in 1301 of Edward I's son, Prince Edward, as Prince of Wales and nominal ruler of the Principality – the first of a long line of English Princes of Wales – facilitated the transfer of Welsh loyalties to the new regime.

Especially in the March, Welsh culture retained its vitality during the fourteenth century. Many of the descendants of English settlers intermarried with native gentry families, so forming a common class with common interests. The period also witnessed a resurgence of Welsh literature, exemplified above all by the poetry of Dafydd ap Gwilym, who flourished from about 1340 to 1370, and who is regarded as Wales's greatest poet.

Dafydd came of an old north Pembrokeshire family. His antecedents had been loyal to the crown for several generations. Dafydd sang of love and fair women, of nature and the beauties of the Welsh countryside. He typified an entire class of Welsh poets which in earlier times had relied on the patronage of the princes. But with the events of 1282, 'the poetry of the princes' became 'the poetry of the *uchelwyr*', as the poets now sang to their new patrons.

Implicit, rather than explicit, in the attitude of these Welsh court poets who had transferred their loyalties to the *uchelwyr* was an apolitical attitude of accommodation to English rule. But there was another Welsh poetic tradition which became more relevant to events in Wales as the Edwardian settlement began to crumble later in the fourteenth century. A new period of racial hostility between English and Welsh was now to emerge that was eventually only resolved by Henry Tudor's victory at Bosworth.

The Poetry of Prophecy

Quite different from the tradition of courtly poetry in Wales was the content of the poetry of prophecy (or vaticination). The genre had developed with successive defeats to the Welsh cause in the dark ages and the early middle ages from Anglo-Saxon, Norse, Norman and English invaders.

Drawing its emotional appeal from these reverses, the poetry of prophecy sang of revenge against the Saxons, and of a national deliverer who would restore Welsh fortunes. This deliverer, the Son of Prophecy, was often named after mythical or historical heroes, Cadwaladr, Owain or Arthur. Prophetic poetry was to grow into a considerable literature in Wales as elsewhere in Europe during the middle ages, for the present often seemed infinitely less preferable than the future.

As early as the tenth century, the Welsh poem, *Armes Prydein* ('The Prophecy of Britain') had called for an alliance of the Welsh, the men of Cornwall, the Picts and the Celts of Strathclyde to drive the Saxons into the sea. But the theme of prophecy was projected in its most popular, lasting and sophisticated form in Geoffrey of Monmouth's *Historia Regum Britanniae* or the *History of the Kings of Britain* (1136).

Geoffrey may have been of Breton origin. He was probably brought up in a Norman-Welsh environment at Monmouth; certainly there is a preoccupation in his work with Caerleon-on-Usk, the former Roman legionary fortress twenty miles south of Monmouth. The central theme of the *British History*, as Geoffrey's book is known in its short form, tells of the founding of the British royal line by Brutus, great-grandson of Aeneas, the Trojan hero. Britain was divided at Brutus's death, but his descendants won great victories and even occupied Rome. The sense of Geoffrey's British patriotism is inescapable.

The account of the Saxon invasions of Britain leads to the 'Prophecies of Merlin', which include a vision told by the wizard to King Vortigern of a battle between a Red Dragon, symbolizing the British, and a White Dragon, the Saxons. Initially, the White Dragon is successful, but it is finally beaten by the Red Dragon, Merlin's prophecy of the eventual victory of the British. But King Arthur, who dominates the closing passages of the *British History*, is mortally wounded in civil strife, and carried off to Avalon. Geoffrey also states ambiguously that Arthur's wounds will be 'attended to' in Avalon. He thus leaves open the haunting possibility that Arthur will return to lead the British to victory.

Britain's future is thus uncertain; Cadwaladr, the last British king, is forced to flee abroad, dying in Rome. But an angelic voice reminds Cadwaladr, before his death, of Merlin's prophecies, and adds that 'the British people would occupy the island again at some time in the future, once the appointed moment should come . . .' In this way, the 'Master of Britain' was presented to the medieval world.

After 1282 the poetry of prophecy flourished anew in Wales, dark, obscure and menacing underneath the relatively tranquil decades of the Edwardian equilibrium. Its animal symbolism, with its arcane references to the bull and the bear, the dragon and the lion, may have been based on the 'Prophecies of Merlin' in the *British History*. But in the fourteenth century, in contrast to the following century, prophecy was not related to specific political personalities. Nevertheless, while the court poets in Wales sang of love and nature, a mass of prophetic poetry celebrated revenge against the Saxon, and looked forward to a new time of hope with the arrival of a deliverer.[1]

Social and Economic Crisis

The poetry of prophecy reflected in some ways the ever-present racial tension of fourteenth-century Wales. This tension was underlined in the early 1370s when the English authorities in Wales took security precautions against a landing by Owain Lawgoch, 'Owen of the Red Hand'. He was a direct descendant of the princes of Gwynedd, and a soldier of fortune close to the French court, who claimed to be Prince of

Wales. Owain was assassinated in 1378, and the threat posed by his activities across the water passed.

But of greater significance in the growing racial tensions in Wales as the century progressed was the mounting social and economic crisis. Although origins are uncertain, economic factors such as the contraction of agricultural production, a European phenomenon, were exacerbated by increased taxation following the beginning of the Hundred Years' War between England and France in 1337. During 1348–50 came the Black Death, followed by further outbreaks of the plague in following decades. Altogether perhaps one-third or one-half of the population of England and Wales died. There was a further contraction in trade and agriculture.

Inevitably medieval institutions declined in both the Principality and the March of Wales. In the Principality, English land law was sometimes resented as it led to the escheat, or surrender, of freehold land to the crown in the absence of heirs. Under Welsh law, such property would be divided amongst the family.

As a cash economy spread outwards from the English boroughs, moreover, those landowners bent on expanding their estates would purchase holdings increasingly available under the Welsh system of partible inheritance. This subdivision and purchase of land was a potent influence in weakening the tribal system of common land ownership by the kindred. Other tribal services were commuted for cash, a process begun before 1282. Sometimes escheated land would circulate back to the market for disposal on non-tribal terms.

In the March, where the manorial system had spread into the Mortimer lands on the borders and into Glamorgan, Gower and Pembroke, there was a corresponding decline as feudal services were cancelled for quit rents. Demesne land was sold or let, and there was a gradual emergence of freehold farms. Throughout Wales as the fourteenth century progressed, collective institutions, whether manorial or tribal, were in decline as the emergence of a new landowning class became an established phenomenon. But an increasing burden of taxation was felt throughout society.

In this historic process, the poorest and the weakest went to the wall, becoming landless labourers. War and plague accelerated change, but the tensions in society also increased. In England, these tensions led to the Peasants' Revolt of 1381.

By the closing decades of the century even the Welsh *uchelwyr* were feeling the pinch in a number of ways. They became subject to markedly increased taxation, even if the social crisis meant that they had been able to profit from the misfortunes of the small and poorer landowners. They were increasingly excluded from official and clerical preferment. In addition, the English boroughs in Wales were often insistent in refusing admittance to aspiring Welsh burgesses or purchasers of urban land.

The natural leaders of Welsh society thus found themselves increasingly at the mercy of English officialdom. As we have seen, a *modus vivendi* had emerged earlier in the fourteenth century with the participation of Welsh officials in the governing process. But now, as both feudal society and the Edwardian settlement in Wales disintegrated, renewed national consciousness emerged amongst all classes. At the close of the fourteenth century, political, economic and national resentments in Wales converged to prepare the ground for a historic rebellion, its course indistinguishable from the personality of its leader Owain Glyn Dŵr.

Owain Glyn Dŵr

In the Welsh context, Glyn Dŵr was certainly 'not in the roll of common men'. He was probably born between the years 1354 and 1359, and was descended on his father's side from the princes of Powys; on his mother's side he was directly descended from another Welsh royal family, the princely line of Deheubarth. Through his mother's family, it should be noted, Glyn Dŵr was a cousin of the Tudor family of Penmynydd in Anglesey, from whom ultimately Henry Tudor was descended. He could also claim descent from the princes of Gwynedd through his mother. Glyn Dŵr's princely lineage was thus unique.

Owain held lands in south Cardiganshire through his mother's descent from the dynasty of Deheubarth, but his chief estates, which had once belonged to the princes of Powys, were in north Wales on either side of the Berwyn mountains. These lands he held from the king, by Welsh barony, as a Marcher lord. His two estates were the lordship of Glyndyfrdwy (Glen of the Water of Dee) near Corwen, and Cynllaith Owain (or Sycharth) on the south side of the Berwyns. It was this first lordship that was to give the great chieftain his name of Owain Glyn Dŵr, or Owen of the Glen of Water, anglicized to Owen Glendower.

Owain was educated in the Inns of Court in London, and fought in Richard II's campaign in Scotland during 1385-6, where his military prowess was noted. His wife was Margaret Hanmer, daughter of Sir David Hanmer, one of Edward III's judges, a family of English origin that had become Welsh in attitude. He had a large family of six sons and three daughters, and lived in a comfortable house at Sycharth; his estate was worth about £200 a year, a considerable sum. He was therefore a soldier, a squire and a gentleman who belonged to the Anglo-Welsh aristocracy of the March and who was fully conversant with English upper-class life. As Shakespeare's Glendower tells Hotspur:

> For I was train'd up in the English court
> Where, being but young, I framed to the harp
> Many an English ditty lovely well
> And gave the tongue an helpful ornament.

Shortly before the outbreak of the rebellion, the Welsh poet Iolo Goch sang of Owain's comfortable timber-frame house at Sycarth, 'a baron's court, much frequented by bards, the best place in the world'. There was an adjacent church, heronry, fish pond, deer park and orchard. All this, and much else, was now destroyed in the great rebellion.

Of the rebellion's immediate origins there still remains something of mystery. After years of political crisis, Richard II had been deposed by Henry of Lancaster in September 1399. Some of the Tudor clan in Anglesey had maintained close links with Richard, and perhaps other influential Welshman regretted his removal. But Henry IV, as he now was, had tried to levy the customary taxes which went with the accession of a new monarch, a further source of resentment in Wales. Royal oficials in the Principality, and also their counterparts in the March, were thus apprehensive of riot and sedition in the early months of 1400.

Against this uneasy background, a bitter dispute between Lord Grey of Ruthin and Owain Glyn Dŵr had come to its head in 1400. Owain claimed that Lord Grey had seized without authority some common land on the border of their respective lordships. The Welshman could get no redress from either Parliament or the new king, whose authority was in any case far from established in England. Henry at the same time faced possible hostilities with both the Scots and the French. All these circumstances now led to the Welsh rebellion.

On 16 September 1400 Glyn Dŵr was proclaimed Prince of Wales by a group of associates meeting at Glyndwfrdwy; four days later on 20 September several hundred men under Owain's command sacked Ruthin and attacked other boroughs in north-east Wales including Oswestry, Flint, Rhuddlan and Denbigh. It was the beginning of an upheaval that was only to end with Owain's disappearance in 1415.

Although the English authorities were able to contain the insurrection during the following winter, Owain went over to the offensive in 1401, extending his operations southwards to the Plynlimmon area and to Carmarthenshire in the south. In a letter to the prominent Welsh *uchelwyr*, Henry Dwnn, of Kidwelly, near Carmarthen, Owain claimed to be a deliverer appointed by God to liberate Wales from the English. After years of captivity, the hour of freedom had now struck and only cowardice and sloth could deprive the Welsh nation of victory. It was a theme that was to receive further elaboration by Owain as the rebellion developed from a Marcher dispute into a national insurrection.

Glyn Dŵr's Welsh State

Following the outbreak of the rebellion, Parliament passed in 1401 very strict legislation against the Welsh. No Welshman could be appointed to public service in Wales or acquire property in the English boroughs in Wales and the Marches. The barons of the March were to garrison and equip their castles. Further, even tougher legislation was passed the following year, including an act that castle garrisons were to be not only English, but strangers to the district. Assemblies of Welshmen were proscribed, and the activities of the 'waster, rhymer, minstrel or vagabond' were curtailed, evidence of the role of bards in the insurrection.

Owain's forces now numbered many thousands. During 1402 he captured his old enemy, Lord Grey of Ruthin, who was ransomed for a princely sum. During June 1402 Glyn Dŵr defeated a large English force from the March at Pilleth, or Brynglas, in the lordship of Maelienydd (Radnorshire), a few miles south of Knighton. Many lords of the border were killed and Owain captured Edmund Mortimer, whose nephew of the same name, the young Earl of March, was by the ordinary rules of descent the lineal heir to the crown. Glyn Dŵr moved south, and with local support from the men of Glamorgan and Gwent, attacked Abergavenny, Newport and Cardiff. Soon most of Wales, including the March, was cleared of English forces.

Despairing of release, Edmund Mortimer began negotiations for a common front against Henry IV with the powerful magnate, Henry Percy ('Hotspur'). But in July 1403 Hotspur was defeated and killed by Henry IV at Shrewsbury, so preventing a conjunction of the Welsh and English allies. During this same month Glyn Dŵr took Carmarthen, and advancing eastwards along the Tywi valley seized Dryslwyn and Carreg Cennen castles. Off the coast, Welsh and Breton sailors prevented English resupply of such isolated castles as Harlech, Caernarfon and Beaumaris. Henry IV personally led successive expeditions into Wales but they were defeated by weather, terrain and what was thought to be Owain's necromancy. Shakespeare's Glendower claimed that

> Three times hath Henry Bolinbroke made head
> Against my power: thrice from the banks of Wye
> And sandy-bottom'd Severn have I sent him
> Bootless home and weather-beaten back . . .

During 1404 and 1405 the rebellion came to climax. Harlech and Aberystwyth Castles were captured, so giving Owain a firm territorial base. He summoned a parliament at Machynlleth in 1404, and another at Harlech the following year. He took as his arms the four lions of Gwynedd instead of the single dragon rampant of Powys, and opened negotiations with the King of France as '*Owenys dei gratia princeps Wallie*'. In July 1404 a formal treaty was signed between these two enemies of Henry of Lancaster; at home the panoply of a Welsh state included a clerical bureaucracy.

The following year, 1405, marked the high water mark of Owain's great adventure. In February 1405 Edmund Mortimer, the Earl of Northumberland and Glyn Dŵr agreed to divide England and Wales between them in a 'Tripartite Indenture'. Mortimer was to have southern England and the crown, Northumberland the north, and Owain's greater Wales was to include the English shires west of the Severn and south of the source of the Mersey. The three allies claimed that they were 'the same persons of whom the Prophet speaks . . .'[2]

But the military backing for these dreams was not available. Owain's forces suffered two serious defeats at Grosmont, in the Monnow valley, and at Pwll Melyn (near Usk) in early 1405. In August of that year a French expeditionary force landed at Milford Haven. Carmarthen, Cardigan and Tenby were captured, and a Franco-Welsh force marched through south Wales to Woodbury Hill, eight miles west of Worcester. But a further advance across the Severn into the heart of England was clearly impossible, even if Henry IV was unable to take advantage of the stalemate.

The rebellion still maintained its momentum for another year. In March 1406, at Pennal near Machynlleth, Owain and his chief adherents, lay and clerical, put forward a far-reaching domestic programme. In the context of the papal schism, they agreed to support the French-backed Pope at Avignon in exchange for recognition of a Welsh independent church with a metropolitan see at St Davids. Two universities, one each in north and south Wales, were also proposed. This 'Pennal Policy' complemented Owain's programme for a national parliament with a national church. The alignment with France was similar to the 'auld alliance' between Scotland and France.

But by now the rebellion had passed its zenith, and the chroniclers record that in Gower, in the Tywi valley and in Cardiganshire many of Owain's supporters submitted to the English. Submissions had already been made in Anglesey in 1405. The realists amongst Owain's supporters had begun to abandon his cause, and from now on there was a Lancastrian reconquest of Wales. But Owain still fought on.

How had so much been achieved by Glyn Dŵr? In particular there were two elements in Owain's appeal which enabled him to make the most of his cause. In the first place, the gentry had rallied to his support, providing the military and administrative backing for the revolt. After all, he was one of their class.

One historian, R. R. Davies, has noted that the revolt

began as a conspiracy of a closely-related group of well-to-do gentlemen and throughout its course it was led and sustained by this class of native squires. It was only the experience, both military and administrative, of these men and through their social influence in the localities that the revolt lasted so long and was such a success . . . so it is that the pattern of support for Glyn Dŵr often dissolves into an infinite network of family relationships, extending over several generations and encompassing the whole of Wales in its ambit . . .

It was the power of this interrelated gentry class, exemplified by Glyn Dŵr's Tudor relations in north Wales, or the Dwnns of Carmarthenshire in south Wales, that 'was the foundation upon which the whole structure of rebellion was, of necessity, based'.[3]

This support for Glyn Dŵr by the gentry was not monolithic. Leading Welshmen in both the north and the south opposed his policies, and were never 'out' with Owain. One such was David Gam, a Monmouthshire squire, the ancestor of the Herbert family, who was killed while fighting with Henry V's forces at Agincourt. Another was Glyn Dŵr's own cousin, Howell Sele of Nannau (near Dolgellau). He tried to kill the Welsh leader, according to tradition, but was himself killed and immured in a hollow oak tree, an episode immortalized in Sir Walter Scott's poem *Marmion*:

> All nations have their omens drear
> Their legends wild of love or fear
> To Cambria look – the peasant see
> Bethink him of Glendowerdy
> And shun the spirit's blasted tree.

But on the whole it was the Welsh gentry that provided the backbone of Owain's rebellion. The corollary was that once this self-same class withdrew its support, the rebellion would eventually collapse.

A second cardinal element in Owain's appeal was his skilful use of the ancient prophecies of the Welsh resurgence. This gave the rebellion a historical legitimacy. As early as 1401, outside Caernarfon, Owain had displayed as his standard a golden dragon on a white field. Glyn Dŵr's biographer, Sir John Lloyd, considered that this action would appear to be 'a deliberate echo of that of Uther Pendragon', as described by Geoffrey of Monmouth. Geoffrey had written of Merlin's prophecy, following the appearance of a dragon-shaped meteor, that

Uther would become king. Once king of all Britain, Uther had adopted the name Pendragon, 'Head Dragon', and fashioned a golden dragon standard for use during his military campaigns. The Britons, and later the Welsh, had used the word 'dragon' for many centuries as a euphemism for leader, prince or ruler.

At much the same time, the close of 1401, Glyn Dŵr wrote to Robert III of Scotland for armed assistance on the grounds of common descent from Brutus through Cadwaladr, 'the last crowned king of my people'. Owain had stated that his people were under the tyranny of the Saxons, and had also appealed in much the same terms to the Irish chiefs. The letters were intercepted, but this element in Owain's popular appeal was underlined by his own genealogical descent from the historic Cadwaladr through Rhodri Mawr (the Great) and the line of the princes of Dinefwr.

Owain's invocation of the ancient prophecies was no doubt a matter of belief as much as policy. During the summer of 1403, following his capture of Carmarthen, he summoned a bard named Hopkin ap Thomas ap Einon, of Ynystawe in Welsh Gower. Hopkin was a soothsayer and a 'maister of Brut', of the Brutus version of the British history. His prophecies were couched in the obscure, allegorical language of the *cywydd brud*, the Welsh poetic form which foretold the triumph of the heirs of Brutus.

Brought under safe conduct to Glyn Dŵr, the soothsayer told him that his fate would be capture under a black banner between Carmarthen and Gower. The episode kept Glyn Dŵr away from Gower at this time (the lordship was later devastated). But the story also illustrates 'the spirit of divination and prophecy in which the Welsh leader was so peculiarly at home at all periods of his career'.[4]

Taken together, the resources of the gentry and the influence of the ancient prophecies were thus central to Glyn Dŵr's success. These forces remained for Henry Tudor's invocation in 1485.

Decline and Disappearance

During 1406 Owain's power began to ebb. There were military defeats within Wales, while French troops left the country during the year. The assassination of Philip of Orleans during 1407 removed the leading opponent of Henry IV from the French political scene. English forces in Wales, ever stronger, began using artillery against Harlech and Aberystwyth Castles in 1407, but the garrisons still held out.

Eventually these strongpoints of Glyn Dŵr's principality fell during 1408. Owain's wife and other members of his family were taken at Harlech. With the fall of Harlech, Owain once again became a partisan leader. He staged one last big raid on the Shropshire border in 1410, but some of his senior commanders were captured. These included Rhys ap Tudor of Penmynydd, who was later executed. During 1413 Owain's chief antagonist, Henry IV, died. His son, as Henry V, and immersed in plans for war in France, offered Owain a pardon during 1415.

But acceptance would have destroyed Owain's reputation. By 1415, if not before, Glyn Dŵr had disappeared. One tradition has it that he spent his last days at Monnington Straddel, a secluded manor near Vowchurch in the Golden Valley of Herefordshire, the home of one of his daughters. Another tradition mentions his death on about 20 September 1415. Eventually the King made a grant of pardon to his son, Maredudd, during 1417. By this time the great rebellion was finally over.

What was the rebellion's legacy? The physical destruction in Wales and the Marches was immense; trade and agriculture were affected for at least a generation and over a century later the famous antiquary John Leland noted many ruins in Wales which were said to date from Glyn Dŵr's time. The Lancastrian penal laws became a major source of racial tension.

But, at great cost, Glyn Dŵr had restored Welsh national pride and national consciousness after the decline of the later fourteenth century. He was alone among the earlier figures of Welsh history, in that no bard attempted to write an elegy. This was due not only to the mystery which surrounded his death 'but also to the belief that he had but disappeared, and would rise again in his wrath in the hour of his country's greatest need' (Sir John Lloyd).

The implications of the rebellion are of direct relevance to our story of Henry Tudor. A leading Welsh historian, Glanmor Williams, has written that harsh though the aftermath of the Rebellion might have been, none of the poets blamed Owen. On the contrary, they saw in him the very pattern of their hopes and desires for other Welsh leaders. He had done for Wales what William Wallace and Robert Bruce did for Scotland, or Joan of Arc for France. The patriotism he had inspired did much to account for much of the growing Welsh support at the end of the century for Henry Tudor. Henry's victory in 1485 and his accession to the English throne seemed to many Welshmen to be Owen's belated triumph.[5]

The point of the relationship is made by a story concerning Glyn Dŵr told by the Welsh soldier and writer of Tudor times, Ellis Griffith of Calais. It relates how Owain, walking one day in the Berwyn mountains, met the abbot of Valle Crucis Abbey. 'You are up betimes, Master Abbot,' said Owain. 'Nay, sire,' was the answer, 'it is you who have risen too soon – by a century.'

2

The Silent Revolution

The aftermath of the great rebellion left a legacy of discord and discontent in Wales and the Marches that was to last for generations. Some English garrisons stayed in Wales, but above all there remained the Lancastrian penal code passed in 1401–2.

This legislation prevented Welshmen from exercising the most simple rights of citizenship, including the right of owning property in or near an English borough in Wales or the Marches. Welshmen were prohibited from holding most crown offices and from serving on juries. Englishmen married to Welsh women were to incur all the legal disabilities of the Welsh. A further element in the unhappy legacy of the rebellion was the continuing animosity, amounting almost to a blood feud, between Glyn Dŵr's former supporters and loyalists who had supported the crown. There are many contemporary reports and petitions of the vengeance wrought on loyalists by Owain's men.

But the new national consciousness which Glyn Dŵr had created remained. Owain continued to be celebrated by the poets in many a *cywydd*, an alliterative couplet form, and he was still seen as the deliverer who would one day return.

For many years after the collapse of the rebellion, therefore, Englishmen regarded Wales as a volcano which might at any time again explode into rebellion. This fear was described in *The Libell of English Policye*, composed about the year 1436:

> Beware of Wales, Christ Jesu must us keep
> That it make not our child's child to weep,
> Nor us also, if so it go his way
> By unawareness; since that many a day
> Men have been feared of their rebellion . . .
> Look well about, for God wot we have need . . .

24

Nevertheless, despite the racial animosities and the proscriptions of the statute book, there was a remarkably swift recovery in many ways after 1415.

Partly this was due to the economic revival following the rebellion. Although the destruction wrought by the fighting was real enough, as we have seen, not all parts of Wales were uniformly devastated.

In particular, trade quickly revived from the ports and harbours of south Wales, with Bristol as the commercial centre for wool and agricultural produce. Coasting trade was carried on from smaller harbours such as Kidwelly and the Burry River, but from the larger ports of Haverfordwest, Carmarthen, Swansea and Tenby there was regular passage to Ireland, the Continent and even the Hanse ports. Gradually, some of the restrictions against Welsh burgesses in the boroughs were relaxed.

Moreover, in both the Principality and the Marches, royal officials and baronial magnates continued to find that Welsh deputies were essential for government. From about 1413 onwards, enterprising members of the Welsh gentry took the precaution of obtaining enfranchisement, or denizenship, by Parliament. This gave them the full status of Englishmen, exempt from the penal laws.

Other Welshmen, in considerable numbers, enlisted in the English armies in France, continuing a tradition that extended back to the opening of the Hundred Years' War. Henry V, who as the king's lieutenant in Wales during much of the rebellion had ample experience of Welsh martial ability, enlisted many Welsh captains including David Gam, killed at Agincourt in 1415, and Matthew Goch. The king's retinue included Maredudd ap Owain, the only surviving son of Owain Glyn Dŵr, as well as an obscure squire from Anglesey, Owen Tudor, who during 1420 served in France with Sir Walter Hungerford, the Lancastrian courtier and administrator.[1]

In the Agincourt campaign alone, over 500 Welshmen from Carmarthenshire, Cardiganshire and the lordship of Brecon served under the Chamberlain of south Wales, John Merbury. Thus in the decades between 1415 and the outbreak of the civil wars in the 1450s, a whole class of Welsh men-at-arms returned home from the French wars, their military achievements, their new-found wealth and their self-confidence ritually celebrated by the bards.

Collapse of Royal Authority

All these factors were relevant to the continuing growth of the Welsh gentry class during the fifteenth century. The building of landed estates had begun before 1282, and went on during the fourteenth century. The process had been accelerated by the Black Death and the Glyn Dŵr rebellion. Gradually a modern pattern of landlord–tenant–labourer relationships was emerging out of the erosion of feudalism and the decay of the Welsh tribal system of communal land-ownership.

After 1415 the process continued unabated as landowners in Wales expanded their estates by a variety of means. By purchase and escheat, by lease, marriage and mortgage, and sometimes by force in an age when good land titles were often non-existent, estate building in both town and country continued. Central to this process was the additional leasing of crown land and of such properties as fulling mills which were valuable sources of wealth and privilege. Some of the older estate builders had been granted non-tribal land by the pre-1282 rulers, while some of the newer arrivals invested profit from trade.

But this aspiring landowning class was driven not only by the incentive of economic self-advancement. With the collapse of Owain's rebellion, the leaders of Welsh society resumed their preoccupation with the holding of political office. But paradoxically, despite the defeat of the rebellion English officialdom in Wales increasingly had neither the will nor the power to curb the Welsh gentry as Richard II's officials had done in the closing decades of the previous century.

In an incisive analysis of this development, Glyn Roberts has written that during this period

> a silent revolution went on under the surface. Despite the penal laws of Henry IV, the emergent Welsh gentry steadily gained control over the legal and administrative machinery of the Principality. Throughout the fifteenth century they increasingly acted as deputies to Justices, Chamberlains, and Sheriffs . . .

The pattern was common to the Marches of Wales as well as the Principality.[2] The corollary was that by 1485 an increasingly

independent or autonomous Welsh gentry class was able to rally to
Henry Tudor.

There were several critical factors involved in the virtual collapse of
royal and Marcher authority in Wales during the fifteenth century
which facilitated the emergence of a Welsh landed class.

The first factor of course was the ever-increasing vacuum at the
centre of the English monarchy. Although Henry V's rule in Wales
had its conciliatory aspects he was also firm. In general he maintained,
despite his preoccupation with war in France, the interest in Welsh
administration which his military operations in the country had given
him. Reliable royal officials were appointed to the crown offices, and
the cooperation of the Marcher lords enlisted. The watchword was
efficiency.

The change came with the death of the victor of Agincourt, in his
thirty-fifth year, at Vincennes outside Paris on 31 August 1422. From
1 September 1422 the government of England was carried out in the
name of Henry VI, then barely nine months old. The council which
governed England during Henry VI's minority was a model of
responsibility compared with Henry's own style of rule. But when
Henry declared his minority at an end in 1437, effective exercise of
the absolute powers of the monarchy really depended on the character of the king.

Within a few years increasing debt, conciliar rivalries such as those
between Humphrey, Duke of Gloucester and the Beaufort clan, and the
virtual collapse of the English war effort in France all led to a new crisis
in English political life. By the late 1440s the country was already
drifting towards civil war. In Wales there was an increasing paralysis of
authority compounded by mounting civil disorder.

According to J. R. Lander,

> The potential success of the system lay in the personality of the
> king; on whether he could hold the balance between turbulent men
> too powerful to be ignored, prevent them from gaining undue
> control of his resources in land, men and money, and see that, by and
> large, they used their own in his and general interest. This Henry VI
> conspicuously failed to do.[3]

In general, Henry VI also failed to use the patronage powers of the
crown effectively, with an increasing tendency to appoint ineffective

household officials to royal posts in the Principality of north Wales. The growing tilt in the political balance in favour of Welsh deputies to royal officials was compounded by the wide extent of the royal lands in Wales. This would have made effective supervision difficult even for someone of Henry V's calibre.

In addition to the Principality lands of north and south Wales, the Duchy of Lancaster territories in Wales had become attached to the crown in 1399 with the accession of Henry, Duke of Lancaster as Henry IV. The Duchy included not only the strategically significant lordship of Monmouth and the Three Castles (Grosmont, Skenfrith and White) but the large lordship of Kidwelly, including the commote of Iscennen lying south of the lower Tywi valley.

There were also the separate crown lordships of Builth, Haverford-west and Emlyn. Effective administration of these disparate lands became an insuperable task for a weak monarch presiding over a realm racked by 'lack of governance' as it was known in contemporary language.

The fragmentation of political power in the Marches of Wales was even more marked. Increasingly from the late fourteenth century, many of the most important lordships became part of magnate conglomerations that included lands in England and sometimes Ireland. The lordship of Glamorgan, held by the Earl of Warwick, 'the Kingmaker', in the mid-fifteenth century, and also the county of Pembroke, owned by Humphrey, Duke of Gloucester for decades before his death in 1447, came into this category.

Other Marcher conglomerations, such as the Mortimer inheritance ruled from Ludlow, and the lordships of the Staffords, who owned Brecon, Hay and Huntington, as well as Newport, were affected by minorities during the early fifteenth century. In these circumstances, effective Marcher government over lordships with differing customs was at a discount. The whole edifice of royal and Marcher rule in Wales as it had existed since 1282 was crumbling.

This disintegration of authority was further exacerbated by the endemic financial crisis of the Principality and the Marcher lordships following the destruction of the rebellion. Both the rulers of the Principality, especially in south Wales, and many of the Marcher lords now used their judicial privileges to raise money by suspending or even cancelling the annual great sessions (or sessions in eyre). In exchange for this abrogation of the judicial process, Welsh communities had to pay a stiff fine. The process was politically significant in that a major concession had now to be offered to the Welsh by the authorities involved; in the latter decades of the fourteenth century the taxes would have been imposed without any concession. Now this was impossible.

Although this fund-raising device was profitable in financial terms, its effect on the maintenance of law and order in a country already racked by chronic lawlessness may be easily imagined. Moreover, not only was justice bartered for cash, but the virtual judicial abdication by royal and Marcher rulers was balanced by a corresponding increase in the effective local power of the Welsh gentry.

'The willingness of Henry V to offer reconciliation to the Welsh gentlemen was succeeded by the inability of Henry VI to do otherwise,' writes Professor Ralph A. Griffiths, an authority on the period:

> Whereas Henry V recognized that such men were needed to govern their localities, collect the king's revenue, and ensure the cooperation and peacefulness of the community as a whole, Henry VI's reign saw the government even surrender its control over these gentlemen. Thus, the opportunity for them to recover their prewar position in society and government was soon transformed into an opportunity to construct a society in which they alone predominated and in which they could defy even the English king. Largely through the appalling weakness and paralysis that overtook local government during the fifteenth century, gentlemen were able to rise to a position never obtained before since the Conquest – and despite the fact that many of their class had participated in the bloody rebellion barely a generation earlier.[4]

The Crisis of the Old Order

The rise of the Welsh gentry in this manner was facilitated not only by the paralysis of royal (and Marcher) authority, but by the unique scale of the lawlessness in Wales and the Marches. In England during the same period, the collapse of royal authority encouraged the growth of local, regional rivalries and 'bastard feudalism'. This was the system by which nobles enlisted retainers in their service by contract (or indenture) in exchange for a cash payment. The rivalry between the Nevilles and the Percys in the north of England, for example, is a prime example of the escalation of private feud into public warfare during this period.

But in Wales, the erosion of authority was compounded by the lingering animosities of Glyn Dŵr's rebellion and resentment of English boroughs and English burgesses who stuck by the letter of the Lancastrian penal legislation. The violence engendered by these resentments affected not only the Marches proper but parts of the adjacent English counties of Shropshire, Hereford and Gloucester.

The communal violence was facilitated by the ease with which malefactors could escape to the Marches with their mosaic of independent jurisdictions. According to Howell T. Evans, as early as 1442

> the blaze of riot raged with amazing fury, private property and public finance equally involved in the general ruin. It was found impossible to arrest miscreants. They passed from one lordship to another and . . . transferred their ill-gotten wealth to places of security and themselves beyond the reach of law and justice.

In a famous account of the period detailing the breakdown of the old order, Sir John Wynn of Gwydir (d. 1627), near Conwy, wrote that 'in those days and in that wild world every man stood upon his guard, and went not abroad but in sort and so armed as if he went to the field to encounter with his enemies'.[5]

Neither the royal administration in the Principality nor the Marcher lords could control violence on this scale. Helped by this collapse of normal restraints, effective political and economic power on the local level continued to pass to the Welsh gentry. The paradox of this breakdown in society lay in the fact that it was an important side of the process in which the squirearchy of later medieval Wales rose to both power and relative wealth. It was this class which provided the social foundation which Henry VII (and his successors) found to be their primary support in Wales.

Of this process Glanmor Williams has written:

The rapid disintegration of the old order in the first half of the fifteenth century enabled the up-and-coming families to build their fortunes much more quickly than would otherwise have been possible. A decisive phase in the origins of the landed families who dominated pre-industrial Wales is almost always to be traced to the first half of the fifteenth century. This was the time when the Herberts, the Salusburys, the Bulkeleys, the Wynns, the Mostyns and the rest, got the boost, which raised them above the ruck, no matter how imposing the pedigrees, real and fictitious, that were subsequently blazoned for them . . . So fluid were political and economic conditions at the outset that the most successful families could hope to come to the very top, and that within a generation almost . . .[6]

The fifteenth century was also a time of great danger as well as of great opportunity to the ambitious, given the unusual hazards that attended politics. Success and fortune, once obtained, could be quickly lost along with life itself.

Henry Tudor was the most prominent beneficiary of the troubles of the fifteenth century. But his father, Edmund Tudor, died at Carmarthen following his capture by Yorkist forces in 1456, and his grandfather, Owen Tudor, was executed at Hereford following the Lancastrian defeat at Mortimer's Cross in February 1461. Jasper Tudor, Edmund's brother, providentially escaped capture and almost certain death on several occasions during the civil wars. The survival of Henry Tudor himself, whether in exile or in battle, was in doubt up to the moment of victory at Bosworth. It was a high-risk age for the leaders of the various factions involved.

A striking example of the dangers inherent in these 'fluid political conditions' is found in the career of William Herbert, Earl of Pembroke. He was the son of Sir William ap Thomas, 'the Blue Knight of Gwent', and Gwladys Ddu, daughter of the celebrated Welsh commander, David Gam, killed at Agincourt in the service of Henry V.

In 1440, Herbert was described as a mere 'chapman'. But during the 1450s, as the rivalry between York and Lancaster deepened into civil war, Herbert obtained favour from both sides. In particular, during this decade, he became both the Duke of York's steward of Usk, Ewyas Lacy and other Marcher lordships and Warwick the Kingmaker's sheriff of Glamorgan. Herbert's intimate knowledge of the southern

March and his ability to raise local forces was thus a critical element in his rise.

Although the subject of Lancastrian overtures, Herbert's basic sympathies were Yorkist, and after the rebel victory of Northampton (1460) he rallied to Duke Richard. Herbert was at the side of Edward, Earl of March, during the Yorkist victory of Mortimer's Cross in February 1461. He was by now one of the senior Yorkist advisers who met in London early the following month and who decided to proclaim Edward King on 4 March 1461.

Decisive preferment followed. Herbert was made a baron, the first Welshman to enter the English peerage, excepting Henry VI's uterine brothers, Edmund and Jasper Tudor, who had been granted earldoms in 1452. Herbert was also made justice and chamberlain of south Wales, as well as a member of the King's inner council. As we will see later in our story, Welsh poets hailed William Herbert as a 'Son of Prophecy' who would free Wales.

Edward IV's wish to create a new court party resulted in Herbert's accumulation of more power than any Welshman since the conquest. His son was betrothed to Mary Woodville, the Queen's sister, in 1466; by then this scion of the Gwent gentry was amassing an English magnate income of over £2,000 per annum.

Following the fall of the last Lancastrian stronghold of Harlech in 1468, Herbert was awarded Jasper Tudor's forfeited earldom of Pembroke. But the wheel of fortune had revolved too quickly for Herbert. With a new round of the civil wars in 1469, his predominantly Welsh forces were defeated at the Battle of Banbury. Summary execution followed on the orders of Herbert's former patron and later rival for Edward IV's favour, Warwick.

Founding Fathers: Penrhyn and Dinefwr

William Herbert's fall was an exception to the remarkable self-preservation and self-advancement displayed by many of the more prominent Welsh gentry during the fifteenth century. The founders of two families in particular underline this point. In north Wales, Gwilym ap Gruffydd was the effective founder of the Griffiths of

Penrhyn, near Bangor. In south Wales, Gruffydd ap Nicholas of Newton (Drenewydd), near Llandeilo, was the founder of the Rice family of Dinefwr. In both cases, the rise of these families is involved with the broader story of the Tudors.

Gwilym ap Gruffydd (d. 1431) was a kinsman of the powerful Tudor clan of Penmynydd, Anglesey, first cousins of Owain Glyn Dŵr. He inherited land at Penrhyn, the nucleus of the family estate, and during the 1390s held various crown offices in Anglesey, becoming sheriff in 1396–7. His first marriage was to a daughter of Goronwy ap Tudur, the brother of Maredudd ap Tudur, father of Owen Tudor. Both Gwilym and the Tudors were descended from Ednyfed Fychan (d. 1246), seneschal or steward to Llewellyn the Great.

The Glyn Dŵr rebellion was enthusiastically supported by the Tudors, and it appears that at first Gwilym ap Gruffydd joined the rebels. But in 1405, as the tide began to turn, Gwilym submitted to the King, receiving formal pardon in 1407. His forfeited lands were returned to him, together with lands of other rebels in Anglesey. By 1410 he was also granted the forfeited lands of Rhys and Gwilym ap Tudur, his wife's uncles, who remained loyal to Glyn Dŵr. Rhys ap Tudur, meanwhile, was captured and probably executed at Chester in 1412.

Not long after, Gwilym built a residence at Penrhyn; a second marriage to Joan, daughter of Sir William Stanley of Hooton, had already opened the road to further power and influence. One probable effect of Gwilym's possession of the Tudor lands in Anglesey was the departure of Owen Tudor to the service and later the court of Henry V. When Gwilym died in 1431, his considerable estates in Anglesey and Caernarfonshire were left to his son by his second marriage; part of the original Tudor estates at Penmynydd was inherited by his first son. But this branch of the family declined into relative obscurity.

Gwilym ap Gruffydd's son, grandson, and great-grandson added to the great Penrhyn estate. His son became deputy chamberlain of north Wales, while Gwilym's grandson and great-grandson were both appointed chamberlain.

Gwilym's grandson was appointed chamberlain of north Wales by Richard III in 1483. The appointment was renewed by Henry VII one month after Bosworth Field, and thus Gwilym ap Gruffydd and his immediate descendants 'served Henry IV, V, and VI, Edward IV, Richard III and Henry VII without ever making a false step'.[7]

Perhaps even more remarkable than the steady consolidation of the Penrhyn estate despite all dynastic changes was the meteoric rise of Gruffydd ap Nicholas of Newton (d. 1460), grandfather of Sir Rhys ap Thomas. In Welsh legend, Gruffydd's family was descended from Urien Rheged, a sixth-century British prince of Strathclyde. Urien's son, Owain, was reputed to have a bodyguard of fierce ravens, hence the three black ravens in the heraldic arms of Gruffydd and his descendants and the family motto, 'God Feeds the Ravens' (*Duw gatwo'r brain*).

The Tudor genealogist, Lewis Dwnn, considered that Gruffydd ap Nicholas was descended from Goronwy ab Einion, lord of the Welsh commotes of Kidwelly and Iscennen, lying south of the lower Tywi valley. Gruffydd's grandfather was Philip, son of Sir Elidir Ddu, a Knight of the Holy Sepulchre, while his father, Nicholas ap Philip, may have died before Gruffydd's birth.

This Nicholas lived at 'a simple howse' at Crug, near both to Llandeilo and to Dinefwr Castle. He married Jennet, the daughter of a local crown official. She was also the grand-daughter of the Welsh magnate, Llewellyn Foethus ('the luxurious') of Llangathen, a parish lying immediately to the west of Dinefwr. Nicholas's brother, too, seems to have held office locally either at Carmarthen or across the Tywi in the nearby Duchy of Lancaster lordship of Kidwelly. Gruffydd ap Nicholas, who was probably born in the last decade of the fourteenth century, thus came of an old Welsh gentry family.[8]

The holding of crown office was thus normal in this family, whatever the Lancastrian penal statutes decreed. But the abnormal circumstances following the Glyn Dŵr rebellion meant that an exceptionally ambitious – and sometimes unscrupulous – Welsh official could win and hold high office in a way unknown since the conquest.

This was the context of the career of Gruffydd ap Nicholas. By 1425 Gruffydd was King's approver for royal demesnes at Dinefwr, and by 1436 (if not earlier) he was sheriff of Carmarthenshire. The following year he was granted denizenship and also acted as deputy justiciar at Carmarthen Castle in the place of Lord Audley, a most significant promotion. There was also the steady accumulation of freehold and leasehold land in both Carmarthenshire and the lordship of Kidwelly. In 1439 Gruffydd was granted a sixty-year lease of the royal castle, town and lands of Dinefwr. This, of course, was an unusually long lease.

Gruffydd ap Nicholas's attitude to central authority was exemplified by the fate of a royal commissioner, Sir Robert Whitney, who had been sent to west Wales in about 1441 to curb the already endemic lawlessness. At Llandovery, Gruffydd himself had met Whitney. But the royal emissary and his fellow-commissioners were soon surrounded by Gruffydd's armed retainers as they proceeded to Carmarthen via Abermarlais and Newton.

At Carmarthen, the commissioners told the mayor and bailiffs to arrest Gruffydd. But during supper, the newcomers were 'soe well liquor'd' that they forgot their mission, and Gruffydd was able to steal the King's commission. The next morning, the commissioners were unable to proceed against Gruffydd, who accused them of being 'traytours and imposters'. They were hurried off to jail, and only released when they agreed to put on Gruffydd's 'blew coat and weare his cognizance' and admit their offence to the King.

When Humphrey, Duke of Gloucester became justiciar of south Wales in 1440, Gruffydd acquired a powerful new patron. Gloucester died after arrest at the Parliament of Bury St Edmunds in 1447, and although Gruffydd was briefly imprisoned following these events, he was soon released and quickly transferred his loyalty to the new justiciar in south Wales, Lord Powick. He thus continued to act as deputy justiciar in Carmarthen. To the absentee rulers of the Principality of south Wales and of the lordship of Kidwelly, Gruffydd was by now indispensable.

Ralph A. Griffiths writes

By the late 1440s he had virtually supreme control of the government of the Principality in south Wales, accounting in his own name to the Exchequer for its revenue . . . holding the highest courts of justice and supervising castle-building and repairs. He communicated directly with the Council at Westminster and advised on the issue of commissions to preserve the peace in Carmarthenshire and Cardiganshire . . . whilst the King addressed him as 'right trusty and well-beloved friend'.[9]

The zenith of Gruffydd's power came in the early 1450s. By now he had probably taken over Carmarthen Castle as a residence, while he, his family or his close associates held effective authority in the key west Wales castles of Aberystwyth, Cardigan, Kidwelly and Carreg Cennen, high on a limestone crag east of Llandeilo. On the site of the 'new town' of Dinefwr, Gruffydd built a manor house. This hall (or *neuadd*), known as Newton, was praised by the poets for its hospitality and patronage. Gruffydd is further recorded as having summoned, and presided over, a great meeting of bards at Carmarthen in about 1453; metric rules were revised and new regulations promulgated.

Gruffydd ap Nicholas has been described as a man 'verie wise', and 'infinitlie subtle and craftie, ambitiouse beyond measure, of a busie stirring braine';[10] he was married three times to wives from leading west Wales gentry families. Through these strategic marriages, his estates and influence continued to grow.

Following the onset of the Wars of the Roses with the first Battle of St Albans in 1455, Gruffydd's power began to wane. First Yorkist forces entered west Wales, to be followed by a resurgence of the Lancastrian presence. Gruffydd had supported the Lancastrian regime because its very weakness magnified his power. But now, in the late 1450s, Gruffydd was overshadowed by Jasper Tudor's presence in Pembroke.

Gruffydd ap Nicholas probably died in 1460. Although the family's political ascendancy in west Wales declined with the advent of the Yorkist regime in 1461, Gruffydd's patrimony had by now been too firmly established to be affected by mere dynastic change. Through his son Thomas ap Gruffydd the mantle of power and authority descended to his grandson, Rhys ap Thomas.

Rhys ap Thomas chose the right side in 1485, becoming Henry Tudor's leading, indispensable Welsh adherent whose career marked the apotheosis of the Welsh gentry in the later middle ages. In this way, the life of Sir Rhys ap Thomas, KG, justice and chamberlain of south Wales, signified the final triumph of the 'silent revolution'.

3

The House of Tudor

Who were the Tudors? Before, during and after Henry Tudor's march through Wales in 1485 he drew vital support in that country from his British descent in general and from his family connections with the old Welsh ruling families in particular.

His descent from the dynasty of Deheubarth, according to the genealogies, extended his line back through Rhodri Mawr (d. 878) and Cadwaladr (d. 664) to the origins of the kingdom of Gwynedd in the fifth century. So Henry Tudor could claim a connection with the oldest ruling families in Welsh history.

Geoffrey of Monmouth's *British History* with its emotive, legendary significance attached to the Trojan line and to Cadwaladr, 'the last British king', added to Henry's appeal and put the Tudor claims to the crown into a context which transcended the dynastic rivalries of York and Lancaster. Henry Tudor was saluted by the bards as a British king in the true line of Brutus and therefore worthy of all possible Welsh support.

As we shall see later in our story, the Yorkists too, in the person of Edward IV, were hailed by such influential bards as Lewis Glyn Cothi. He was a poet who went on to support Henry Tudor, so returning to his first allegiance, the Lancastrian cause. But Edward, Earl of March, later Edward IV, had a claim to Welsh loyalties through his descent from Gwladys Ddu, Gwladys the Dark (d. 1251). She was a daughter of Llewellyn the Great who married Ralph Mortimer of Wigmore. The line then descended through the Mortimers to Richard, Duke of York, Edward IV's father, who was killed at the Battle of Wakefield in 1460.

There was no inconsistency in the bardic change of allegiance to differing Sons of Prophecy. Their loyalty was to the most effective champion of Welsh interests and not to the rival claims of York or

Lancaster. But as became evident by 1485, Henry Tudor, through his descent from Owen Tudor, and the family's involvement with Owain Glyn Dŵr, had special claims to Welsh allegiance.

Ednyfed Fychan

The use of the word 'Tudor' (Welsh for Theodore) as a family surname only began in the fifteenth century. But the origins of the family are generally acknowledged to lie with Ednyfed Fychan, or Ednyfed ap Cynwrig, seneschal or steward to Llewellyn the Great of Gwynedd and his son David from about 1215 to his death in 1246. Ednyfed was tenth in descent from Marchudd, the head of the clan known to genealogists as the Eighth 'Noble Tribe' of north Wales. The tribal territory was found in the area later known as Denbighshire.

Ednyfed Fychan was an experienced and possibly outstanding administrator. He was richly rewarded by the princes of Gwynedd with special grants of land which sustained the family fortunes until adherence to the cause of Owain Glyn Dŵr brought an end to the main line of the family centred at Penmynydd, Anglesey.

Especially significant for the later cause of Henry Tudor was Ednyfed Fychan's marriage to Gwenllian, daughter of the Lord Rhys of Deheubarth (d. 1197). The Lord Rhys – or Rhys ap Gruffydd – was the last King of Deheubarth, ruling from Dinefwr, who claimed independent regal rights. In agreement with Henry II about 1158, he surrendered his regal claims, and was henceforth known as 'the Lord Rhys'. Following this homage to the English king, however, the Lord Rhys was able to reclaim much of the historic territory of Deheubarth lost to marauding Marcher lords such as the Cliffords and the Clares. Under him, this reconstituted Deheubarth reached its greatest extent and thus his descendants enjoyed great prestige.

But this prestige was not merely a matter of politics. Rhys ap Gruffydd was descended directly from the line of Rhodri Mawr, King of all Wales, a descendant of Cadwaladr and Cunedda. Lord Rhys's mother was Gwenllian, daughter of Gruffydd ap Cynan of Gwynedd, while his wife was another Gwenllian descended from the princes of Powys.

In this way, the descendants of Ednyfed Fychan and Gwenllian could claim kinship with all three royal families of Wales. While the Tudors were descended from Ednyfed's son, Goronwy, another of the seneschal's sons, Gruffydd, was the ancestor of the mother of Rhys ap Thomas of Dinefwr. There was thus a kinship between Henry Tudor and his chief Welsh supporter on the road to Bosworth.

For his political and military services to Llewellyn the Great of Gwynedd, Ednyfed Fychan the Seneschal was awarded lands within the principality. The unique tenurial concession was also made that all descendants of Ednyfed's grandfather (Iorwerth ap Gwrgan) should hold their lands throughout Wales free of all dues and services other than military service in time of war.

Most of the lands concerned were in Gwynedd; but Ednyfed Fychan himself also held small estates outside Gwynedd at Cellan, Llan-rhystyd, and Llandsadwrn in west Wales. This latter holding at Llansadwrn, north-east of Llandeilo in Cantref Mawr, was confirmed by the English crown in 1229. The estate here probably represented marriage gifts made by Rhys Grug, Lord of Dinefwr, to his sister Gwenllian, wife of the Seneschal. In time, this estate at Llansadwrn, with its capital holding or *caput* at Abermarlais, descended to Rhys ap Thomas.

In the years between Ednyfed's death in 1246 and the conquest of Gwynedd by Edward I in 1282–3, his sons continued the family tradition of serving as advisers to the Prince of Gwynedd. Ednyfed's son, Goronwy ap Ednyfed, was thus seneschal to Llewellyn the Last (Llewellyn ap Gruffydd). Goronwy, who died in 1268, was the ancestor of the Tudor family, and he was succeeded as seneschal by his brother, Tudur ap Ednyfed, who died in 1278. But in the case of the third son of Ednyfed Fychan, Gruffydd, there were apparently divided loyalties to the Prince of Gwynedd. Gruffydd's sons, Rhys and Hywel, were on the English side in the campaign of 1277, and Hywel was killed fighting for Edward I in 1282.

By this time, even before the conquest of 1282, the descendants of Ednyfed Fychan formed a powerful clan, comparatively wealthy, and holding their estates by special tenure outside the Welsh tribal system. Their 'widespread possessions, combined with the favourable terms on which they were held, made them the forerunners of that class of Welsh squires whose emergence is characteristic of the post-Conquest period'.[1]

The Tudors of Penmynydd

As we have already seen, this emerging class of Welsh gentry often provided the office-holders in the period after 1282. There were many Welshmen of gentle birth who took advantage of Edward I's proclamation in 1282 that the possessions and privileges of those who submitted to the crown would be undisturbed. Prominent amongst this official class who were to work in conjunction with the crown after 1282 were the descendants of Goronwy ap Ednyfed Fychan, later known as the Tudors.

In a remarkable piece of historical detective work first published in 1951, the late Glyn Roberts described the advancing fortunes of the four successive generations that followed Goronwy ap Ednyfed. These generations lived through the immensely significant period that separated the Edwardian conquest of Wales from the rebellion of Owain Glyn Dŵr. The title of Professor Roberts' famous essay, 'Wyrion Eden' (literally, the grandsons or descendants of Ednyfed) was drawn from the term sometimes used in fourteenth-century documents to describe the special privileges which had been awarded to the family of Ednyfed Fychan, the seneschal of Gwynedd.[2]

The four generations anatomized by Glyn Roberts were those of
1. Tudur Hen (or Senior) ap Goronwy (d. 1311);
2. Goronwy ap Tudur (d. 1331);
3. The brothers Hywel and Tudur ap Goronwy (d. *c.* 1367);
4. The five sons of Tudur ap Goronwy who held estates in Anglesey centring on Penmynydd.

It was one of these five sons of Tudur ap Goronwy, Maredudd, who became the father of Owen Tudor, grandfather of Henry VII. In this way, the blood of Ednyfed Fychan, and Gwenllian, daughter of the Lord Rhys, passed to the 'Royal Tudors'. This was despite the ruin of the original family through their involvement with Owain Glyn Dŵr.

Tudur Hen, the son of Goronwy ap Ednyfed, followed his father in the service of Llewellyn the Last. After 1282, Tudur Hen submitted to Edward I but he may have been involved in the abortive Welsh revolt of Madog ap Llewellyn in 1295. But Tudur Hen seems to have suffered no lasting penalties, and in 1301 he was one of those Welshmen who swore fealty and homage to Edward of Caernarfon, Edward I's son who

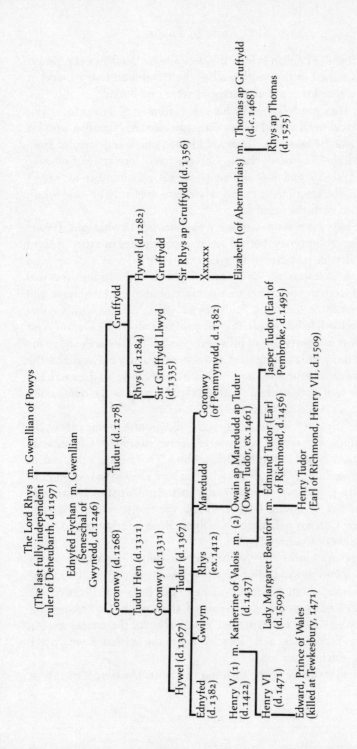

The origins of the Tudors

became the first English Prince of Wales. On his death in 1311, Tudur Hen was buried in the south wall of the Dominican friary chapel at Bangor where his son and grandsons were also buried.

Tudur Hen was followed by his son, Goronwy ap Tudur (d. 1331). He was loyal to Edward II in that unhappy monarch's conflict with his barons, like his kinsman, Gruffydd Llwyd (who was descended from Gruffydd ap Ednyfed Fychan). Goronwy was forester of Snowdon during 1318–19 and was described on his appointment as King's Yeoman. The tradition of crown service was evidently by now firmly established with the family.

In the next generation, Goronwy was succeeded by his sons, Hywel and Tudur ap Goronwy, both of whom probably died in 1367. (A third son, Gruffydd, had died earlier in 1344.) Hywel was a cleric, who became Archdeacon of Anglesey. Together with Tudur, the two brothers were in possession of a number of estates in Anglesey and Caernarfonshire, including Penmynydd with which the family name was henceforth to be linked. This township stands on the shallow crest of the most southerly line of hills in Anglesey. To the north and to the south of this gentle rolling land, the historic granary of Gwynedd, the sea can be seen in the distance. But more significantly, to the south lies the great wall of Snowdonia with its cloud-capped peaks rising quite abruptly, so it seems, from the Menai Straits.

Hywel's brother, Tudur, is of special significance in this part of the family story. His second wife was Margaret, daughter of Thomas ap Llewellyn of Iscoed in south Cardiganshire. Thomas was a descendant of the senior line of Deheubarth who had been allowed to keep some of the family patrimony in west Wales in 1282. Margaret's sister was Elen, mother of Owain Glyn Dŵr. So the five sons of Tudur and Margaret, Goronwy, Ednyfed, Gwilym, Rhys and Maredudd, were first cousins of Owain Glyn Dŵr.

This generation of the five brothers is sometimes known as the 'Tudors of Penmynydd'. But strictly it was the senior son, Goronwy, who inherited from his father, Tudur, the estates at Penmynydd. Ednyfed's lands were found at Trecastell, those of Rhys at Erddreiniog, while the estates of Gwilym were at Clorach. All the estates were in Anglesey, Erddreiniog and Clorach lying to the north of Penmynydd, with Trecastell to the east.

Of the inheritance of the fifth son of Tudur, Maredudd, its precise location remains unknown. Yet he remains genealogically the most significant of this generation. It was Owain ap Maredudd ap Tudur, later known as Owen Tudor, who was Henry Tudor's grandfather, and thus it was Tudur ap Goronwy (d. 1367) who was the immediate ancestor of the royal Tudors, and who gave the dynasty its name.

It was with the sons of Tudur ap Goronwy that the power and influence of the family reached their zenith. Goronwy and Ednyfed died long before the other three brothers. But Goronwy probably fought in France for the king in the Hundred Years' War, and the official positions he held suggest reward for loyal crown service. He was forester of Snowdon, and also steward of the manors of the Bishop of Bangor in Anglesey. A few days before his death in March 1382, he was appointed constable of the imposing Edwardian fortress of Beaumaris Castle, an unusual honour, and a post only once before held by a Welshman.

According to bardic tradition, Goronwy ap Tudur died by drowning in Kent in unexplained circumstances. The same bardic sources state that his body was eventually buried in the Franciscan friary of Llan-faes, near Beaumaris.

At the time of the dissolution of the monasteries, the body of Goronwy and his wife, Myfanwy, were appropriately transferred to Penmynydd church where their splendid alabaster tomb can still be seen. The monument also conveys with considerable power the contemporary importance of Goronwy and carries his arms, a shield charged with a chevron between three closed helmets. But there is no evidence that these arms were used by Goronwy's brother, Maredudd, or by his nephew, Owen Tudor.[3]

Through his daughter Morfudd, Goronwy ap Tudur was the ancestor of the late Tudors of Penmynydd of the sixteenth and seventeenth centuries. But this branch of the family declined into obscurity in contrast to the glittering history of the Royal Tudors.

Goronwy's brother, Ednyfed, died at about the same time (1382) according to an elegy to the two brothers by Iolo Goch (d. 1398). His wife and children, according to the pedigrees, were almost certainly connected with a whole network of influential gentry families in north Wales.

Of the three remaining brothers of the clan, Rhys, Gwilym and Maredudd, the first two were retained by the crown in 1398 for a sum of £10 annually, payable at the exchequer of Caernarfon. Moreover, Rhys and Gwilym may have had some personal relationship with Richard II in the closing years of his reign. But this is not certain. If the brothers were involved with Richard, it would help to explain the alacrity with which they rallied to Owain Glyn Dŵr's revolt against Henry of Lancaster.

The most important of the five brothers in the context of our story, Maredudd, is 'the most elusive'. In Iolo Goch's elegy to Goronwy and Ednyfed mentioned above there is a reference to two of the surviving brothers of the clan, Rhys and Gwilym, but not to Maredudd.

Immediately before 1400, Maredudd was apparently living in north Wales, married to Margaret, daughter of Dafydd Fychan ap Dafydd Llwyd. The birth of their son, Owen Tudor, almost certainly dates to this time. Moreover, in the general pattern of the pre-1400 allegiances of the family, Maredudd was in crown service as escheator of Anglesey in 1392. He also held lands in Anglesey, for, as we shall see, they became forfeit to the crown because of his rebellion.

With the advent of Owain Glyn Dŵr, all three brothers, Rhys, Gwilym and Maredudd, became loyal adherents. R. R. Davies writes:

> The territorial proliferations of 'Wyrion Ednyfed Fychan' and their web of marriage alliances made them into the most powerful family complex in fourteenth-century Welsh politics. Rhys, Gwilym and Maredudd ap Tudur were the scions of this dynasty in 1400, and they brought to Glyn Dŵr's cause their military experience, their prestige, and perhaps above all an impetuous enthusiasm which might have turned into a dangerous degree of independence had it not been for their unwavering loyalty.[4]

From first to last, therefore, the Tudors of Penmynydd were 'out' with their first cousin, Owain Glyn Dŵr. Along with Glyn Dŵr, Rhys and Gwilym were omitted from the pardon given to the original rebels in March 1401. On 1 April that same year, the two brothers with a band of Welshmen captured Conwy Castle. They were pardoned in July 1401, and although this operation at Conwy seems to have been an independent initiative, they remained firmly committed to Owain's cause.

There is a tantalizing glimpse of Maredudd's activities during the rebellion when it is recorded that he was an esquire to Lewis Byford, Glyn Dŵr's Bishop of Bangor, in 1405.[5]

The family involvement with Glyn Dŵr was disastrous. The chronicler Adam of Usk records that Rhys ap Tudur was captured at Welshpool in 1411, and executed with two other Welsh leaders at Chester. Other sources give the date of his death in 1412, and suggest that Gwilym too suffered the extreme penalty. But there is no proof of this and Gwilym may have been given a pardon. It remains probable that Rhys was the only member of the family who suffered death for his involvement with Glyn Dŵr.[6]

Nevertheless, Rhys, Gwilym and Maredudd all lost their lands, forfeited for rebellion. Most of the estates of Rhys and Gwilym passed, as we have seen, to Gwilym ap Gruffydd of Penrhyn. Prior to 1400, Maredudd had also held estates in Anglesey, but with the rebellion they were forfeit, and in 1407 his lands were held by one Richard del Woode. The location and ultimate fate of these lands are not known, but there can be no doubt that Maredudd shared in the general ruin of the family.

A small part of Goronwy ap Tudor's original estate at Penmynydd remained in the possession of his descendants through the marriage of his daughter Morfydd to Gwilym ap Gruffydd of Penrhyn. Some of this land at Penmynydd passed to Gwilym's son Tudur Fychan, by virtue of Gwilym's first marriage to Morfydd. But this was a very small part of the original patrimony, and this branch of the family which continued to live at Penmynydd passed into obscurity.

All the accumulated power and influence of the heirs of Ednyfed Fychan had thus been lost. It was now left to Owain ap Maredudd ap Tudur to re-establish the family in ways undreamt of by his Anglesey forbears.

Owen Tudor

The destruction of the Tudor family fortunes and the passing of their patrimony to Gwilym ap Gruffydd of Penrhyn may well have led Owen Tudor to the court of Henry V. The circumstances in which he entered royal service – like Maredudd, the only surviving son of Owain Glyn Dŵr – remain obscure. Yet this enlistment in the royal service led to the dramatic reassertion of the family which culminated in Owen's grandson becoming King Henry VII. For at some time in the 1420s,

Owen Tudor met and married the Dowager Queen Katherine, widow of Henry V.

Henry V had married Katherine of Valois, daughter of Charles VI of France and Queen Isabella, born into the Bavarian Wittelsbach family, on 2 June 1420. Katherine was then nearly nineteen years of age, and Prince Henry of Windsor, the future Henry VI, was born in December 1421. But on 31 August 1422, Henry V, 'the flower of Christian chivalry', died at Vincennes and Katherine was a widow. According to Professor S. B. Chrimes, Katherine had no part in the government of England during her son's minority, and 'very little share' in his upbringing.

How Owen Tudor came into the immediate service and then the favour of the Queen Dowager again remains unclear. But the link may have been through Sir Walter Hungerford, with whom, as we have seen, Owen Tudor is said to have served in France. Sir Walter had fought at Agincourt, was one of the executors of Henry V's will, a councillor, and from 1424–6 was steward of Henry VI's household. This distinguished Lancastrian soldier and administrator was then made a baron in 1426.[7]

The circumstances that led a lonely young queen to fall in love with the Welsh royal servant are again unclear, but a valid marriage did occur in or about the year 1429. There were four children, Edmund, Jasper, a third son, Owen, who became a Benedictine monk, and a daughter who died in infancy. Edmund and Jasper were probably born during the period 1430–2.

According to Polydore Vergil, writing of the marriage with a certain amount of discretion when Owen Tudor's grandson was on the throne of England:

> This woman after the death of her husband . . . being but young in years and therefore of less discretion to judge what was decent for her estate, married one Owen Tyder, a gentleman of Wales, adorned with wonderful gifts of body and minde, who derived his pedigree from Cadwalleder, the last king of the Britons . . .[8]

During 1432 Owen was given exemption from most of the restrictions placed on Welshmen by the Lancastrian penal statutes of 1401–2. Owen had petitioned the House of Commons for this relief, but there was no mention of his marriage in the petition. Henceforth he was officially regarded 'as if he were a true English subject'.

Katherine became ill in 1436 and was removed to Bermondsey Abbey where she died on 3 January 1437. The body was conveyed to St Paul's and then to the Lady Chapel in Westminster Abbey. Here a tomb was later built by Henry VI.

It was only shortly before her death that Henry VI learnt of his mother's marriage, and Owen probably incurred his displeasure. Owen was now imprisoned during 1437–8, and at some stage escaped from Newgate Prison. He was recaptured and committed to Windsor Castle, but the nature of his alleged offences is not known, and he was given a pardon in 1439. There is no evidence that his imprisonment was connected with his marriage.

Again we lack details of Owen's activities in the years following this episode. But it is known that the King's Council committed the two elder sons of his marriage, Edmund and Jasper ap Meredith ap Tydier, to the care of Catherine de la Pole, sister of the Earl of Suffolk, from 1437 to at least 1440. Eventually these two sons of Owen Tudor, half-brothers of Henry VI, were knighted on 15 December 1449, and then created earls on 23 November 1452. Edmund was made Earl of Richmond and Jasper was made Earl of Pembroke. They were given precedence over all other earls, but no patronymic was used in their creation.

The careers of Owen Tudor's two sons were to take widely differing courses. In 1455 his eldest son Edmund Tudor married Lady Margaret Beaufort (1443–1509), the daughter and heiress of John Beaufort II, Duke of Somerset (d. 1444), and his wife Margaret Beauchamp of Bletso. Somerset was a prominent Lancastrian magnate and a descendant of John of Gaunt (1340–99) and his mistress Katherine Swynford. After their eventual marriage, their bastard, pre-nuptial children had been legitimized by Parliament in 1397 during the reign of Richard II. These children, the Beauforts, were to play a major part in the politics of the fifteenth century.

Through her descent from John of Gaunt, third son of Edward III, Margaret Beaufort was King Edward's great-great-grand-daughter. This was the basis of Henry Tudor's later claim to the throne. But as we shall see later in our story there was continuing doubt over the validity of this claim as King Henry IV had added a rider to the Beaufort legitimization excluding them from the throne.

Edmund Tudor was fighting for the Lancastrian cause in west Wales during 1456 and died in Carmarthen Castle on 3 November of that year. His posthumous son, Henry Tudor, was born in Pembroke Castle on 28 January 1457 when his mother was not yet fourteen years old. With his birth, Henry thus became Earl of Richmond.

Henry Tudor was not wholly Welsh. His grandfather, Owen Tudor, was Welsh, but his grandmother, Queen Katherine, was partly French and partly Bavarian. Henry's father, Edmund Tudor, was thus half Welsh and partly French and German. His mother, Lady Margaret Beaufort, was of course English.

Following the death of Edmund Tudor, Jasper of Pembroke succeeded his brother as Lancastrian lieutenant in Wales and was the life-long guardian of Henry Tudor and his interests. He soon became the mainspring of the Lancastrian cause in general until the final victory at Bosworth, and eventually died in 1495.

From the early 1440s onwards, Owen Tudor achieved ever greater respectability as his career as a Lancastrian stalwart became established. During these years he was variously called Owen ap Meredith ap Tudur, Owen Meredith, Owen ap Meredith, and Owen ap Tuder. In his petition to the Commons in 1432, he called himself Owen ap Meredith, and his pardon of 1439 was made to Owen Meredith.

Finally, Professor Chrimes has noted, the choice of his surname was made by the crown. From 1459, he was called Owen Tudor Esquire; on 19 December of that year Owen was granted an annuity of £100 from estates confiscated from John, Lord Clinton, and in February 1460 he was granted the office of parker of the King's Parks near Denbigh. Owain ap Maredudd ap Tudur had thus become Owen Tudor. It was in this way that England came to be ruled not by a Meredith but by a Tudor dynasty.[9]

Following the Lancastrian defeat at Mortimer's Cross near Presteigne on 2 February 1461 Owen Tudor was captured and executed at Hereford. But Owen's death and Jasper's continued activities on behalf of the House of Lancaster underlined Henry Tudor's later claim to the throne through his mother, Margaret Beaufort.

Owen had also re-established the prestige of the Tudor family in Wales. The family could justly claim to be descended from the old

48

princely families and also from the most famous adviser of the rulers of Gwynedd. The Tudors had suffered and lost nearly all in the Welsh national cause under Glyn Dŵr. These claims were destined to evoke a historic response when Henry Tudor landed in Wales in 1485.

4

War in Wales

The new national awareness created by the Glyn Dŵr rebellion and the gradual consolidation of a Welsh gentry class was underlined after the early 1450s by the outbreak of civil war, the Wars of the Roses. To many in Wales the struggle between York and Lancaster was less a dynastic struggle than an opportunity for advancing Welsh national interests.

But the political crisis of Henry VI's reign took time to develop into open warfare. Even then the campaigning was sporadic rather than intense. The first open military clash came with the Battle of St Albans in May 1455. Eventually, after another half-decade of increasing turmoil, the Yorkist challengers discovered that replacing Henry VI's advisers and even capturing his person were inadequate objectives. With the installation of Edward of March as Edward IV in 1461, the crown itself was the price of the contest.

During a quarter of a century the throne changed hands six times and three of the five monarchs involved – Henry VI, Edward V and Richard III – died violent deaths. Moreover, the families of both York and Lancaster were eliminated in the direct male line. Out of this prolonged crisis of civil war and dynastic revolution, Henry VII was to emerge as both victor and beneficiary.

In the course of these extraordinary events, many Welsh poets hoped that somehow a leader would emerge who would free Wales. The Lancastrian Jasper Tudor was cast in this role, as was the Yorkist William Herbert. These bardic prognostications were well founded. The Wars of the Roses were a serious, prolonged crisis for the English monarchy. The course of events was quite unpredictable.

In addition, the control of Wales and the Marches came to be of great importance for both York and Lancaster, so increasing the leverage of those who could appeal to Welsh sentiment. G. M. Trevelyan has written that the Wars of the Roses were to a large extent a quarrel among Marcher Lords. For the great Lords Marcher were closely related to the English throne and had estates and political interests in both England and the Welsh March. Harry Bolinbroke of Hereford and Lancaster was a great possessor of Welsh lands, as also were his rivals, the Mortimers. The House of York, Warwick the Kingmaker, and Richard III's Buckingham were all in one way or another con-connected with Wales and the Marches.[1]

The Yorkist Challenge

At first, the importance of Wales as a pivot of hostilities was subordinated to the political challenge posed to Henry VI's administration by Richard, Duke of York. During 1450 York had vainly attempted to remove Edmund Beaufort, Duke of Somerset (d. 1455) and other controversial figures from the royal household by parliamentary action.

Two years later, as the factional struggle grew ever more intense, York had tried to impose his will by force on the King, but again he miscalculated. During this episode, York was faced with a stronger royal army at Dartford outside London. Before he was allowed to return home to Ludlow Castle, the 'capital' of the Yorkist Marcher Lordships, he was humiliatingly forced to take a public oath that he would not instigate another rising.

York's actions in 1450 and 1452 were impelled by both political and personal considerations. He was no doubt concerned with the growing maladministration inseparable from Henry VI's rule. But York was not only a great magnate with particular interests in Wales and the Marches, he also believed that he had a better legitimist claim to the throne than Henry VI.

York's father, Richard, Earl of Cambridge, was descended from Edmund of Langley, the first Duke of York, and fourth son of Edward III. (John of Gaunt, named after the anglicized form of his birthplace, Ghent, and ancestor of the House of Lancaster, was the third son of Edward III.) But York's mother, Anne Mortimer, was descended from Lionel of Clarence, second son of Edward III. There were no formal precedents, and York made no explicit claim until 1460, but if the female claim were allowed, his title to the throne was better than that of Henry VI. In any case, York was heir presumptive to the throne from 1447 to 12 October 1453, when Queen Margaret gave birth to Henry VI's son and heir, Prince Edward. This fact underlined his unspoken interest in the succession.

Despite his setback in 1452, York was not a man to give up, and events during 1453–4 moved in his favour. In August 1453 Henry VI suffered a complete mental collapse and eventually York was appointed Protector in April 1454. His Protectorate lasted until February 1455. During this period York not only controlled the administration but was able to extend his political influence by allying himself with the Nevilles, probably the most powerful political clan in the country. This alliance between the House of York and leading members of the Neville family was a central theme in events for the next fifteen years.[2]

The family had been founded by Ralph Neville, first Earl of Westmorland (d. 1425), whose second marriage to Joan Beaufort, daughter of John of Gaunt, produced twelve children and brought the family close to the House of Lancaster. The eldest son of the marriage, Richard Neville, Earl of Salisbury (d. 1460) had acquired his earldom as a result of his marriage with the heiress Alice Montague. His sister, Cicely Neville, meanwhile, married Richard, Duke of York, with whom Salisbury was eventually to become politically allied.

Salisbury's son, also named Richard Neville, acquired great wealth and influence through his marriage to Anne, heiress of Richard Beauchamp, Earl of Warwick. In 1449 Neville himself was made Earl of Warwick and from that year he was in possession of the rich lordship of Glamorgan. Warwick also acquired the lordships of Abergavenny and Elfael in the Welsh Marches. His role in the forthcoming civil war was to earn him the title of 'the Kingmaker'. But in general, as events were to show, Warwick's ambition was somewhat greater than his military ability.

Prior to 1450, the Nevilles had been allied to the Lancastrian regime, but regional conflict with the Percy family in the north of England, who were supported by Henry VI, estranged them from the court. Warwick had also quarrelled with Edmund Beaufort, Duke of Somerset, York's chief adversary in government. So in this way York and the Nevilles were drawn together. Their combined territories in

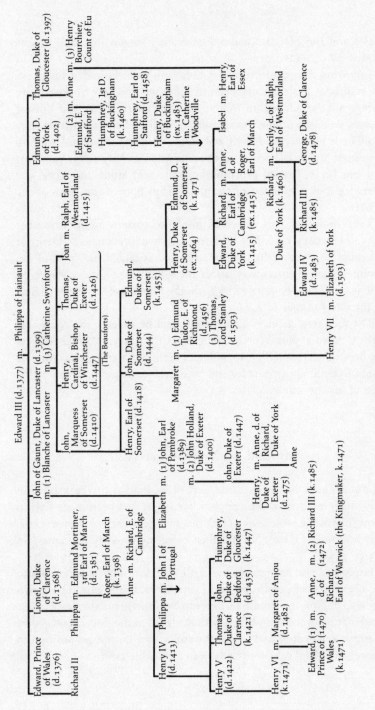

York and Lancaster

Wales and the Marches had a significant military potential, as was soon to be demonstrated.

Following Henry VI's recovery of his sanity at the end of 1454, and the ending of York's Protectorate in February 1455, the Yorkists were once again excluded from influence at the court. When the Yorkist leaders were summoned to a royal council at Leicester which they thought would demand their complete submission, political warfare developed into a clash of arms at St Albans on 22 May 1455. Somerset and the Percy Earl of Northumberland were killed and York and Warwick took possession of the King. Thus opened the Wars of the Roses.

There followed York's second, brief Protectorate from November 1455 to February 1456. But York was unable to sustain his influence at the court, as most of the influential barons regarded Henry VI as the anointed King. Increasingly under the influence of Queen Margaret, who was implacably opposed to York, the King moved to the Midlands in the late summer of 1456.

The area was strongly Lancastrian, and henceforth the court was mostly based at Kenilworth Castle, near Coventry. Normal political life became increasingly impossible as both Lancastrians and Yorkists began to build up support for the coming confrontation. This was the setting for the war in Wales.

Edmund Tudor in West Wales

Edmund Tudor had been made Earl of Richmond (in Yorkshire) in November 1452. His younger brother Jasper had been made Earl of Pembroke at the same time. The titles and legitimacy of the two earls, half-brothers of Henry VI, had then been confirmed by Parliament in March 1453.

Jasper had also been given the castles and lordships of Cilgerran, to the north-east of Pembroke, and Llanstephan to the east. The crown lordship of Emlyn, adjoining Cilgerran, was also granted to Jasper. The combination of these lordships with the lands of the Royal Principality in south Wales appeared to put the crown in a favourable position in the region. Pembroke especially was a valuable asset.

The County Palatine of Pembroke, with which Jasper was now to be associated in one way or another for the rest of his life, comprised the southern portion of the later county of Pembrokeshire created by the Act of Union of 1536. Pembroke Castle, with its massive walls and towers, and with its great cylindrical Norman keep, was considered virtually impregnable and had never been taken by the Welsh. The fortress overlooked a long, narrow walled town standing on a limestone ridge between two tidal arms of Milford Haven, a site ensuring resupply by sea even if the castle were invested.

But despite Jasper Tudor's grant of Pembroke and other lordships in west Wales, and successive efforts by the Lancastrian government to curb the endemic lawlessness in the area, effective control of the area remained with Gruffydd ap Nicholas and his family. Gruffydd's attitude to central authority remained that of over a decade before when he had bundled back to London a royal commissioner wearing his coat and cognizance.

During York's First Protectorate in 1454–5, renewed attempts were made by the government to deal with the anarchy in west Wales. At this stage, apparently, Jasper Tudor probably sympathized with York's policy of reform, which could not of course be enforced in west Wales.

With the Battle of St Albans in May 1455 events in Wales took a significant new course. Edmund Beaufort, Duke of Somerset was killed in the battle and thus York was, for a time, in the ascendant in the government. York was therefore quickly granted Somerset's offices of constable of Carmarthen and Aberystwyth Castles.

Another Yorkist, Edward Bourchier, took over from Somerset as steward of the Duchy of Lancaster lordship of Kidwelly, which on paper should have given York control not only of Kidwelly but of Carreg Cennen Castle. This latter stronghold was a look-out for the lower Tywi valley and guarded the important strategic route from Hereford and Brecon through Llandovery to Carmarthen. Yet another Yorkist, Sir Walter Scull, had been officially constable of the royal castle of Cardigan for some years.

York's grant of Carmarthen and Aberystwyth Castles was apparently underlined with his Second Protectorate during the winter of 1455–6. But in fact all the five principal castles of west Wales, Carmarthen, Aberystwyth, Kidwelly, Cardigan and Carreg Cennen, remained in the hands of Gruffydd ap Nicholas, his sons Owain and

Thomas, or of their follower, Rhydderch ap Rhys. The overall picture was not altered by York's grant early in 1456 of Dinefwr Castle and its demesnes to Sir William Herbert of Raglan, so displacing Gruffydd ap Nicholas from this important lease. It seemed as if the decrees of Lancastrians and Yorkists alike could not be enforced in west Wales.[3]

In early 1456 Edmund Tudor was sent to west Wales by the court party. His Welsh extraction and his close relationship with the King could be expected to rally support in an area where there was considerable Lancastrian sympathy. Nominally, the crown position seemed strong, in that the two counties of the Royal Principality in the area, Carmarthenshire and Cardiganshire, as well as Jasper Tudor's lordship of Pembroke, were considered loyal to Henry VI. The lordship of Brecon was also ruled by a crown supporter, the Stafford Duke of Buckingham. In addition Kidwelly was crown territory as part of the Duchy of Lancaster. The crown also controlled the three counties of the Royal Principality in north Wales, centred on Caernarfon.

On the other hand, York held the Mortimer lordships of the March, governed from Ludlow, which cut off the crown territories in Wales from England. An almost solid block of Yorkist lordships included Usk, Caerleon, Ewyas Lacy, with its *caput* at Longtown, Builth, Radnor, Wigmore, Maelienydd and Denbigh in north Wales. The lordships of Ceri, Cydewain and Montgomery were also under York's control. In general, Wales was thus divided between Lancaster and York, with the former predominant in the west, the latter in the east. York's ally, Warwick, as we have seen, controlled Glamorgan. From the court's viewpoint, the problem of Yorkist influence in Wales was not simply a territorial one. The Mortimer lordships along the March were an easy recruiting ground for a soldiery long inured to warfare.

The campaigning in west Wales following Edmund Tudor's arrival soon developed into a three-cornered contest between Edmund, Gruffydd ap Nicholas and Yorkist forces. Edmund Tudor was in Pembroke during the early months of 1456, and on 7 June it was reported to John Paston that Edmund and Gruffydd ap Nicholas were 'at war greatly in Wales'.[4] Edmund also took over Carmarthen Castle of which York was technically the constable.

As in the Welsh wars of Edward I and Glyn Dŵr's campaigns, Carmarthen was the key to west Wales, including Pembroke. The royal castle, a stone-built structure on the site of an earlier Norman

Wales and the Wars of the Roses

ANGLESEY
Beaumaris
Conwy
Caernarfon
CAERNARFONSHIRE

Rhuddlan
Flint
FLINT
CHESTER
Chester
Denbigh
DENBIGH
Ruthin
RUTHIN
(Grey)
Holt
BROMFIELD & YALE
Chirk
Blore Heath X

MERIONETHSHIRE
Harlech

Oswestry
OSWESTRY
(Arundel)
Shrewsbury
Severn

POWYS
(Powys)
Welshpool
Caus
CAUS
CYDEWAIN
Dolforwyn
Montgomery
CLEOBURY-
MORTIMER
CERI
Clun
Ludlow
Cleobury
Richards
Castle

Aberystwyth
CARDIGANSHIRE

MAELIENYDD
Wigmore
Wigmore

CWMWD
DEUDDWR
Mortimer's
Cross X

Radnor
Huntington

BUILTH
ELFAEL
Builth
(Warwick)
Painscastle
Clifford
Hereford
Wye

Cardigan
Cilgerran
Newcastle
EMLYN
(Pembroke)
Llandovery
Brecon
Ewyas Lacy

Newport
CEMAES
(Audley)
CARMARTHENSHIRE
Dryslwyn
Dinefwr
BRECON
(Buckingham)
Grosmont
Skenfrith
Abergavenny
ABERGAVENNY
(Neville)
Monmouth

PEBIDIOG
(Bishop of St D.)
St David's
Wiston
(Bishop of St D.)
Carmarthen
Carregcennen
GWYNLLWG
(Buckingham)
Usk
CHEPSTOW
(Norfolk)
Caerleon

Haverford
Narberth
(Devereux)
Laugharne
Kidwelly
KIDWELLY
(Lancaster)
GOWER
(Norfolk)
Swansea
GLAMORGAN
(Warwick)
Newport

PEMBROKE
(Pembroke)
Tenby
Llanstephan
Pembroke

Cardiff

LANCASTER
Lands of the Crown
Lands of Lancastrian supporters
YORK
Lands of the Duke of York
Lands of Yorkist supporters

0   10   20 miles

building, was the centre of government for the southern part of the Royal Principality of Wales. Routes ran north, south, east and west to Cardigan, Swansea, Brecon and Pembroke respectively.

Carmarthen comprised both an 'old town' held by an Augustinian priory and a 'new town' immediately outside the walls of the castle. There was a Franciscan friary. Placed at the head of navigation of the Tywi, it was the most populous and richest town in Wales, with many trading links to Bristol, London and the Continent. The castle, which had been repaired for the princely sum of £380 after twice having fallen to Glyn Dŵr, contained not only the offices of the justice and chamberlain of south Wales, but a chapel, a granary, an exchequer and many other amenities. Five round towers and an elaborate gateway (which still survives) were only part of Carmarthen Castle's fortifications.

Acquisition – and retention – of this prize would be of great importance to the Yorkists. Evidently the Duke of York now decided to pursue his claim as constable of both Carmarthen and Aberystwyth Castles and to contest Edmund Tudor's influence in the region. During August 1456 Sir William Herbert of Raglan and Sir Walter Devereux of Weobley, Herefordshire, two of York's tenants and loyal supporters in the Marches, advanced on west Wales with a column of 2,000 men from Hereford and nearby Marcher territories.

Carmarthen Castle was besieged and captured by the expedition and Edmund Tudor imprisoned. The Yorkist forces then moved northwards to seize Aberystwyth. The archives in the two castles and the seal of the chamberlain of south Wales were taken. To emphasize the validity of York's claim, Herbert and his men issued a commission to themselves to hold the great sessions, although Gruffydd ap Nicholas had presided over these courts during the previous May. The Yorkist justices were later stated to have released all those summoned before them. By this use of force, York had made his claim as formal representative of the legal government in west Wales.[5]

Gruffydd ap Nicholas, now faced with both royal and Yorkist forces in west Wales, evidently decided to make his peace with the Lancastrians. In the autumn of 1456 Queen Margaret was travelling through the Welsh border areas, and on 26 October full pardon was granted to Gruffydd and his two sons, Owain and Thomas, for all treasons, felonies and other crimes committed by them. From now on

Gruffydd and his family supported the Lancastrian cause in Wales.

Edmund Tudor, meanwhile, had died at Carmarthen on 3 November 1456, but it remains unclear whether his death was connected with his imprisonment by Herbert's forces. He was buried at the Greyfriars, the house of the Franciscan Friars which stood immediately west of the town walls; the tomb was moved to St David's Cathedral at the time of the dissolution. On 28 January 1457, less than three months after Edmund Tudor's death, his wife, Lady Margaret Beaufort, gave birth to his son, Henry Tudor, at Pembroke Castle. With his birth, the future Henry VII became the Earl of Richmond.

Jasper Tudor's Tenby Base

Although Edmund Tudor's death removed the chief Lancastrian leader in the region, York's campaign for the control of west Wales had not succeeded. Herbert's forces could not be sustained in the area and instead there was a growing consolidation of royal rule under the strong personal leadship of Edmund's brother, Jasper Tudor. Gruffydd ap Nicholas and his family now took second place to the King's half-brother.

Illustrating the new balance of power in west Wales, Jasper was formally awarded the castles of Carmarthen, Aberystwyth and Carreg Cennen in April 1457. The Duke of York was stated to have relinquished the constableships of these castles at the King's wish, receiving instead a grant of £40 per annum.

While the Countess of Richmond and her baby son remained at Pembroke Castle, Jasper himself now established both a headquarters and a base at Tenby, about ten miles east of Pembroke on the shore of Carmarthen Bay.[6] The town here was more convenient for Jasper's purposes than Pembroke Castle. In an earlier period, Tenby had been taken by the Welsh at least twice, in 1187 and 1260. The new walled town and its castle had successfully withstood a siege by Glyn Dŵr and his French allies in 1405, but since that time nothing had been done to improve the fortifications.

Jasper now moved quickly to take maximum advantage of Tenby's small but deep-water harbour, sheltered on the lee shore of his lordship, which gave passage to both England and to north Wales, Scotland, Ireland and France. It was from this harbour that Jasper and his nephew, Henry Tudor, were to escape to Brittany after what seemed the final collapse of Lancastrian hopes in 1471.

A still extant letter from Jasper to his mayor and burgesses of Tenby dated 1 December 1457 makes a series of specific grants for the strengthening of Tenby's fortifications. In particular, the burgesses were empowered to make the walls six feet thick and the moat thirty feet across. Time was evidently of the essence as Jasper also empowered the mayor 'to impress carpenters, masons, and other workmen anywhere in the county of Pembroke, and to pay them at statutory rates'.[7] The work was carried out to such good effect that many of Jasper's fortifications remain visible, especially Tenby's great west wall and its arched gateway which still dominates much of that salubrious town.

As a result of Jasper's activities, Lancastrian rule in west Wales was unchallenged for the next two years.

The Fight for the Throne

During 1458–9 Jasper Tudor as the leading Lancastrian in the area continued to build up support for the King in Wales and the Marches. Jasper was now increasingly hailed by some poets as a champion of Welsh national interests. One of the most influential of these bards was Lewis Glyn Cothi whom we shall meet again in our story. During 1457–8 the poet praised Jasper for his Welsh extraction, his royal descent from Queen Katherine and his efforts to unite Wales for the King. Doubtless the poet's praises for Jasper were not unprompted, as in the Welsh bardic tradition a poet's loyalties were directly related to his patron's politics.

One of the patrons of Lewis Glyn Cothi was Gruffydd ap Nicholas who, with his family, was now firmly allied to the Lancastrian cause. On 1 March 1459 Jasper and Owen Tudor and the two sons of Gruffydd ap Nicholas, Owain and Thomas, were commissioned to arrest certain Yorkist supporters in west Wales, including some of the servants of John Dwnn of Kidwelly, a leading Yorkist in the region.

On the wider political scene, Lancaster and York were as far apart as the factions in west Wales. Despite the so-called 'Loveday' of 24 March 1458 when rival leaders marched arm-in-arm to St Paul's Cathedral, while thousands of their armed retainers were stationed in nearby streets, the interests of the court and of the Yorkist leaders were irreconcilable. But what brought about the final rupture was the decision by Queen Margaret to eliminate her opponents by force.[8]

A royal council met at Coventry in June 1459 to which the Yorkist leaders were not asked. Threatened by indictments from this council, the Yorkists planned to confront the King, but first to concentrate their forces at Ludlow. Part of this strategy involved the Earl of Salisbury, Warwick's father, marching south from Middleham in Yorkshire to join York. On 23 September 1459 crown forces, directed by Queen Margaret, attempted to intercept Salisbury's men at Blore Heath in north-east Shropshire. The royal forces were worsted, there were relatively heavy Lancastrian casualties, and Salisbury continued his march to Ludlow.

Three weeks after Blore Heath, the Yorkist and Lancastrian armies faced each other across the Teme at Ludlow on the night of 12 October. The Lancastrians were led by the King, and taking advantage of a royal pardon, York's forces on the south side of the river at Ludford Bridge faded away. York fled through Wales to Ireland, while Salisbury, Warwick and York's eldest son, the young Edward, Earl of March, escaped to Calais. Warwick had been captain here since 1455 despite all attempts by the court to displace him.

When Parliament met at Coventry in November 1459, the Yorkist leaders were attainted. They were thus declared rebels and all their lands and possessions forfeit to the crown. This development was decisive in that Yorkist leaders could now only achieve their objectives by force. In the Welsh Marches, the victorious Lancastrians took over Yorkist lordships and their castles, a process that culminated in Jasper Tudor's seizure of Denbigh, a Mortimer fiefdom, in March 1460.

York at Dublin and Warwick at Calais now carefully coordinated their plans which resulted in Yorkist forces from Calais landing at Sandwich in Kent on 26 June 1460. London welcomed the stability which it thought a Yorkist regime would bring, and in any case the court had long removed its presence (and patronage) to the Midlands.

But the prerequisite of Yorkist success was military victory and possession of the King's person. This was achieved by the Yorkist forces at Northampton on 10 July 1460. Queen Margaret fled through Cheshire to Harlech and thence to Pembroke Castle. She then sailed to Scotland, leaving Jasper to mobilize the Lancastrians in Wales for the next phase of the struggle which was to culminate in the Battle of Mortimer's Cross the following February.

Richard, Duke of York had remained in Ireland during the campaign that culminated in the victory of his supporters at Northampton. Then in September 1460 he landed near Chester and advanced through Shrewsbury and Hereford to London with the undisguised objective of claiming the throne. Previously he had borne only the arms of York; he now blazoned the royal arms of England, claiming the crown though his descent from Lionel of Clarence, second son of Edward III.

Reaching London in early October, York went to Westminster Hall where he laid hand on the empty throne to the silent disapproval of the assembled Lords of Parliament. When Archbishop Bouchier asked if he would like to go and see the King, York made his famous reply: 'I know of no person in this realm the which oweth not to wait on me, rather than I on him.' But the Lords would not support his wish that Henry VI should be deposed in his favour.

Eventually a compromise was reached. On 24 October 1460 Parliament passed an Act of Accord which recognized Henry VI as King for life, but disinherited his son, Edward, Prince of Wales, and placed the succession in the person of York and his sons. York's bid for the throne was now close to success. Although York had been named as Protector, Queen Margaret refused to accept her son's disinheritance. York would still have to fight before the succession to the throne was his.

Mortimer's Cross

Despite this triumph, York faced a formidable Lancastrian coalition which was determined to destroy him. By December Queen Margaret was at Hull, supported by an array of Lancastrian barons from the north and west of England. But success was contingent on coordination between these forces and those being mobilized by Jasper Tudor in Wales. York, meanwhile, had reached Sandal Castle, near Wakefield, by Christmas, while his son, Edward, Earl of March was at Shrewsbury rallying Yorkist forces on the Welsh border.

On 30 December 1460 the fight for the throne entered its last and bloodiest phase. York and his second son, Edmund, Earl of Rutland were killed in the Battle of Wakefield. They had been outwitted by local Lancastrian forces. Salisbury was executed after capture and York's head wearing a paper crown placed on the gates of the City of York. During January a Lancastrian army headed south for London from York, plundering and pillaging as it advanced. Yet for a final, decisive Lancastrian victory over the Yorkist armies, it seemed essential for Jasper Tudor's forces to defeat their enemies in the Welsh Marches and link up with Queen Margaret. Then London would have to capitulate.

This seems to have been the Earl of Pembroke's strategy. By January 1461 Jasper had mobilized a force of Welsh, Irish and French troops under his leadership and that of the Earl of Wiltshire. The latter had probably landed at Milford Haven at the very close of 1460 with levies from his Irish estates. This combined force now moved north-eastwards along the Tywi valley and over the hills through Builth towards northern Herefordshire. The winter weather as this Lancastrian force crossed the watershed between the Tywi and the Wye could hardly have improved its efficiency.

From Presteigne the Lancastrians moved six miles eastwards towards Leominster and ultimately the Severn crossing at Worcester. Here they found they were facing a Yorkist army, mustered at Hereford, at Mortimer's Cross on the River Lugg. In command was Edward, Earl of March. Battle was inevitable between the rival leaders and their two armies composed on both sides of forces chiefly drawn from Wales and the March.

On 2 February 1461 the Yorkists under the eighteen-year-old Edward of March won the day. Little is known of this decisive encounter apart from a strange portent appearing in the heavens, for

> there were seen three suns in the firmament shining full clear, whereof the people had great marvel, and thereof were aghast. The noble Earl Edward them comforted and said, 'Be of good cheer, and dread not; this is a good sign . . .'[9]

From this portent of Yorkist victory, Edward later took a favourite personal badge, the Sun in Splendour.

Jasper Tudor and Wiltshire escaped from the field of Mortimer's Cross. But Owen Tudor, who had accompanied the Lancastrian forces on the march through Wales, was captured and taken to Hereford. There he was put to death:

> And he was beheaded at the Market Place, and his head set upon the highest grise of the market cross: and a mad woman combed his hair and washed away the blood of his face, and she got candles and set about him burning, more than a hundred. This Owen Tudor was father unto the Earl of Pembroke and had wedded Queen Katherine, King Henry VI's mother, weening and trusting all the time that he would not be beheaded, till he saw the axe and the block; and when that he was in his doublet he trusted on pardon and grace till the collar of his red velvet doublet was ripped off. Then he said, 'That head shall lie on the stock that was wont to lie on Queen Katherine's lap'; and put his heart and mind wholly unto God, and full meekly took his death.[10]

The Yorkist victory at Mortimer's Cross was to have a significant effect on the course of the war. Queen Margaret had defeated Warwick's Yorkist forces at the second Battle of St Albans on 17 February 1461. But the news of the Lancastrian army's pillaging on the way south had stiffened the resolution of London not to admit the Queen's forces. Henry VI had been recaptured by the Lancastrians at St Albans, and after some hesitation outside London, the Queen and her reunited husband now withdrew to York.

London instead opened its gates to the victorious Yorkist forces of Edward, Earl of March, who had of course succeeded his father as Duke of York on the latter's death at Wakefield the previous December. With Henry VI's person now repossessed by the Lancastrians, there was evidently no alternative now in the Yorkist strategy to having March proclaimed and installed as King Edward IV on 4 March 1461.

It should be remembered that York and his colleagues had three times in the past six years dominated the royal administration, but only as a result of the King's incapacity or capture in battle. After York's First Protectorate of 1454–5 the King had recalled advisers hostile to York. The same had happened after the first Battle of St Albans and York's brief Second Protectorate during 1455–6.

The Yorkists had recaptured the King again after the Battle of

Northampton in 1460, but the Queen had fought on and now, with the second Battle of St Albans in February 1461, the royal figurehead had been won back by the Lancastrians. Even if Henry VI were taken again by the Yorkists, there was no certainty that they could rule in his name as his chief adviser was no other than Queen Margaret, the leading enemy of the Yorkists. Events thus led the Yorkists to proclaim their own king and so establish beyond dispute their own regal legitimacy, provided they could convincingly defeat the Lancastrian forces.

The basis of the Yorkist claim to the throne, Charles Ross has written in his biography of Edward IV, 'lay in the concept of legitimate inheritance'. As set forth in a petition from the Commons in Edward's first parliament (November 1461), his claim emphasized that because the Lancastrian kings had all been usurpers, by God's law, man's law, and the law of nature, the right title lay in Edward, as heir of Lionel of Clarence, after the death of his father, Richard, Duke of York. Moreover, continuing Lancastrian resistance before 4 March 1461 had breached the Parliamentary Act of Accord of October 1460. For these reasons the usurper, Henry VI, had been removed, and the 'rightwise and natural liege and sovereign lord' of Englishmen had resumed possession of his inheritance.

Decision at Towton

Edward of March, meanwhile, was in a very strong position after his victory at Mortimer's Cross, not least because Warwick's influence had inevitably been devalued as a result of his defeat at the second Battle of St Albans. The army which provided the military sanction for Edward IV's installation as King in Westminster Hall was a personal Yorkist force which had been largely recruited from the Mortimer lordships of Wales and the Marches.[11]

Edward IV now acted with great speed and resolution. He quickly organized fresh Yorkist forces and moved north to confront the Lancastrian army at Towton, about ten miles south-west of York, on 29 March 1461. The smashing Yorkist victory on that day proved to be the biggest battle of the Wars of the Roses. Henry VI and Queen Margaret fled to Scotland, and although sporadic Lancastrian resistance continued in Northumberland for three more years, Edward IV's position was unchallenged until the end of the decade. The Yorkist succession was thus underwritten by the decisive victory won by Edward at the Battle of Towton.

There remained a year's campaigning ahead in Wales. Pembroke and Carreg Cennen Castles were to yield to the Yorkists. Harlech's Lancastrian garrison did not surrender until 1468. But in Wales as a whole the Yorkist victory was soon complete.

5

Yorkist Victory

The Battle of Towton in March 1461 was followed by a consolidation of Yorkist rule through England and Wales. After the battle which effectively confirmed the dynastic revolution earlier in the month, Edward IV returned to London for a formal coronation at the end of June 1461.

There remained a prolonged mopping-up operation to be organized in Wales. The task was given by Edward to William Herbert of Raglan, who now became the mainstay of the Yorkist regime in Wales and a valuable counterweight to Warwick at Edward IV's court. As we have already seen, Herbert was at Edward's side when the sun burst double at Mortimer's Cross. As one of the small group of Yorkist advisers who had decided to proclaim Edward king in early March 1461, Herbert was now given unprecedented authority for a Welshman.

In May 1461 he was made justice and chamberlain of south Wales, steward of Carmarthenshire and Cardiganshire and constable of Dinefwr Castle. When Edward was formally crowned at the end of June, Herbert was made a baron, the first member of the Welsh gentry to enter the English peerage. He was then summoned to Parliament with this rank in July 1461. Along with Herbert, his Marcher colleague Sir Walter Devereux of Weobley was also made a baron as Lord Ferrers of Chartley.

Other prominent Yorkists were given key positions in Wales. Lord Hastings was made chamberlain of north Wales, and the Earl of Worcester the justice. Lord Grey of the Marcher lordship of Powys was given the stewardships of the border lordships of Ceri, Cydewain and Montgomery. The veteran Yorkist John Dwnn of Kidwelly was created constable of Carmarthen and Aberystwyth, and sheriff of Carmarthen and Cardiganshire.

These grants to loyal and reliable Yorkists had more than local significance. The Yorkist victories of 1461 and Edward's assumption of the throne meant a major shift in the balance of power in Wales against the Marcher lords. After 1461 the two sections of the Royal Principality, the Duchy of Lancaster lands and the Mortimer inheritance were all held by the crown. Warwick held Glamorgan and Brecon was at the disposal of the crown during the minority of the heir to the dukedom of Buckingham. Jasper Tudor's county of Pembroke was also forfeit. The crown was thus in a relatively stronger position in Wales than at any time since the conquest of 1282.

Pembroke Castle Surrenders

This was the political background in 1461 to the Yorkist expedition into Wales with the objective of removing the last remnants of Lancastrian resistance. In particular, three Lancastrian castles remained unsubdued: Pembroke, Carreg Cennen and Harlech.

The first objective was to seize Jasper Tudor's county of Pembroke. Following Herbert's appointment as justice and chamberlain of south Wales, he and his brothers had been given a commission to take into the King's hands Pembroke and other lordships held by Lancastrians in west Wales. A further commission was issued to Herbert and Lord Ferrers in August 1461 to array forces from the border counties of Hereford, Shropshire and Gloucester. The following month the King moved to Ludlow.

Pembroke Castle was soon to fall. A small Yorkist fleet was sent to Welsh waters to prevent Lancastrian reinforcement by sea. Following Herbert's demand, Sir John Skidmore delivered the castle on 30 September 1461 'without any war or resistance'. Such a surrender without a long siege was customary in the Wars of the Roses, although the Castle was amply provisioned. Tenby also surrendered to Herbert despite all the care lavished on the fortifications by Jasper Tudor.[1]

Jasper, however, had escaped from Pembroke to north Wales, where the local Lancastrians made a last stand at Tuthill, outside Caernarfon, in October 1461. Once again, Jasper eluded his Yorkist adversaries, and, fleeing through Ireland, reached Scotland where the Queen had retreated after Towton. Further adventures in France and Brittany lay ahead and he was not destined to return to Pembroke for nearly a decade.

Following the surrender of Pembroke Castle, William Herbert acquired further rewards from a grateful Edward IV. Jasper Tudor's earldom of Pembroke and his other possessions were declared forfeit in November 1461. Three months later, in February 1462, Herbert was granted custody of Pembroke, Tenby and the other west Wales lordships of Cilgerran, Llanstephan and Emlyn formerly held by Jasper. The town and castle of Haverfordwest were also placed in his hands.

At the same time, February 1462, Herbert was given custody of the large lordship of Gower which now became a valuable link in the Yorkist control of west Wales, situated as it was between Kidwelly and Warwick's lordship of Glamorgan. Throughout the middle ages and until the Act of Union of 1536, Gower and its appendage, the Manor of Kilvey, were quite separate from the lordship of Glamorgan. Rather, its links were with the wider history of west Wales. As Herbert was also the royal justice at Carmarthen, these connections were again underlined.

The former Lord of Gower, the third Mowbray Duke of Norfolk, had not sided with the Yorkists until immediately before Towton in March 1461. During the following November Duke John II of Gower died and Edward IV decided to put the lordship into the custody of Herbert during the minority of Duke John's son. There were good security reasons for this decision.

Not all the Gower gentry had followed the late Duke in his change of allegiance from Lancaster to York. Lancastrian supporters in Gower included Philip Mansel of Oxwich and Hopkin ap Rhys of Llangyfelach, both of whom had fought at Mortimer's Cross. After joining further Lancastrian conspiracies both were attainted in 1465 and their lands given to a kinsman of Herbert's, Sir Roger Vaughan of Tretower.[2]

These grants, together with his other offices in the Principality of south Wales, gave Herbert virtually vice-regal powers in the region. He was now ready to reduce the last local Lancastrian stronghold, Carreg Cennen Castle. This fortress was held by Owain and Thomas, the sons of Gruffydd ap Nicholas, who had escaped from the field of Mortimer's Cross. Carreg Cennen controlled the commote of Iscennen in the lordship of Kidwelly, so its acquisition was clearly necessary to the Yorkists.

In April 1462 Herbert's younger brother, Sir Richard Herbert, and Sir Roger Vaughan of Tretower arrived at Carreg Cennen with the mission of ending Lancastrian resistance there. Owain and Thomas were persuaded to surrender. Carreg Cennen was then garrisoned by Yorkist troops during the summer of 1462 'for the safeguard of the same, forasmuch as the said castle was of such strength that the misgoverned men of that country there intended to have inhabited the castle and to have lived by robbery and spoiling of our people'. However, in August 1462 it was decided to demolish the Castle 'to avoid inconvenience of this kind happening there in future'. Some 500 men 'with bars, picks and crow-bars of iron and other instruments necessary for the same purpose' were engaged on the work of demolition at a cost of £28 5s. 6d.[3]

With this 'slighting' ended the effective life of Carreg Cennen. Yorkist control over west Wales was complete.

Harlech Castle in Merionethshire continued to hold out. This Edwardian stronghold, rich in its associations with Glyn Dŵr, provided a link with Lancastrian exiles in Scotland and France. Yorkist garrisons in north Wales had to be maintained, moreover, as a result of the latent threat posed by this obstinate Lancastrian force.

At the same time, Edward IV must have realized that a set-piece siege of this remote, almost impregnable fortress would be enormously expensive. So Welsh poets continued to sing the praises of Harlech's defenders, and only in 1468 was the fortress reduced by William Herbert. This proved to be Herbert's last military success.

Tudor and Herbert

Of Henry Tudor's early life little remains known. But what is probable is that following his birth on 28 January 1457, the first fourteen years of his life were spent in Wales, mostly under the guardianship of William Herbert, the leading Welsh Yorkist.

Henry came under Lord Herbert's guardianship soon after the surrender of Pembroke Castle on 30 September 1461. The four-year-old Earl of Richmond and his mother, Lady Margaret Beaufort, were then captured by Herbert's forces. As we have seen, Henry's uncle, Jasper Tudor, the leading Lancastrian in Wales, became a political fugitive with the fall of Pembroke.

The fortunes of war meant that Henry Tudor's life took a completely new direction. By February 1462 his custody and right of marriage had been sold by the crown to William Herbert for £1,000. In August of that year Henry was deprived of his title of Earl of Richmond. The child was probably soon separated from his mother, for at some time before 1464 Lady Margaret married Henry Stafford, the second son of Humphrey, first Duke of Buckingham. Stafford died in October 1471 and his wife then married Thomas, Lord Stanley, the Cheshire magnate, before October 1473.

With the fall of Pembroke Castle, Henry Tudor's life for almost a decade was thus part of the Herbert household. Following Herbert's creation as a baron in June 1461, he had been granted the following February the custody of Pembroke and the other west Wales lordships once held by Jasper Tudor. This custody had been granted from 4 March 1461, the beginning of the Yorkist era with the accession of Edward IV.

In all probability Henry Tudor therefore continued to live at Pembroke Castle under the immediate care of·Herbert's wife, Ann Devereux, sister of the Yorkist Sir Walter Devereux, Lord Ferrers of Chartley. Some of Henry Tudor's boyhood was also spent at Herbert's home at Raglan Castle. But Henry's latest biographer, Professor Chrimes, notes

> that there is no evidence that he went outside Wales at all during this period, or at any other period, until the flight to Brittany in 1471, except perhaps for the visit to London with Jasper during the period of the Readeption.

(The Readeption of Henry VI took place from 3 October 1470 to 11 April 1471.)

Henry Tudor was therefore brought up in Wales. Good tutors were provided, he was treated according to his birth, and Lord Herbert hoped to marry him to his daughter, Maud. His future thus seemed inseparable from that of the leading Welsh Yorkist family, and his marriage and career would no doubt have the approval and patronage of the Yorkist King.[4]

As the decade advanced, so William Herbert continued to find royal favour not only as the virtual Yorkist ruler of Wales but as a leading member of the court party which was designed to counter the influence of Richard Neville, Earl of Warwick. In 1462 Herbert was made a KG and during 1463 Edward IV created a new Marcher lordship for Herbert by detaching territories from around Crickhowell and Tretower in the Mortimer lordship of Blaenllyfni, part of the Yorkist earldom of March. Two years later, the Marcher lordship of Raglan was created for Herbert from the land of the Yorkist lordship of Usk. Meanwhile, the King's marriage to Elizabeth Woodville in 1464, and extensive provision for a family widely regarded as upstarts by the traditional peerage, continued the consolidation of the court party.

Herbert's influence was further advanced when in September 1466 his son and heir, William, was married to the Queen's sister, Mary Woodville, at Windsor with great ceremony. Herbert's son was given the title of Lord Dunster. The following year, in August 1467, Herbert was made justice of north Wales – he already held the position of justice of south Wales, as we have seen – and as steward of the lordships of Brecon, Builth, Caerleon, Ceri, Cydewain, Denbigh, Montgomery and Usk he dominated the Marches as well as the Principality. His income, at over £2,400 per annum between 1465–8, had now reached English magnate status.[5]

The campaign of 1468 in north Wales brought Herbert's extraordinary career to its zenith. During June of that year Jasper Tudor, accompanied by a small group of adherents, landed from Normandy on the coast of north Wales, probably near Barmouth, and advanced as far as Denbigh. The Castle did not surrender, but the indefatigable Lancastrian leader was apparently able to hold sessions at Denbigh in the name of Henry VI. The hapless Lancastrian king, meanwhile, had been captured after the final collapse of his supporters' resistance in Northumberland in 1464, and was lodged in the Tower.

Faced with this challenge in north Wales, Edward IV acted with his customary despatch. Lord Herbert was commissioned to array the Welsh Marches as well as the adjacent English shires against Jasper. Herbert then advanced northwards from Pembroke to Harlech, while his younger brother, Richard, pushed southwards up the Conwy

Plate 1   a. Pembroke Castle. Birthplace of Henry Tudor
and stronghold of his uncle, Jasper Tudor.

b. Mill Bay, Pembrokeshire.
Henry Tudor's landing place, 7 August 1485.

Plate 2
a. Lady Margaret
Beaufort. Artist
unknown, late sixteenth
century.
b. Tomb effigies of Henry
VII and Elizabeth of York
by Pietro Torrigiano,
c. 1512-19 (*Westminster
Abbey, Henry VII
Chapel*)

Plate 3   King's College Chapel, Cambridge. A great shrine of the 'Tudor Myth'.
a. Tudor heraldry. The Beaufort Portcullis, the Tudor Double Rose, and the Greyhound and the Dragon.
b. The royal arms of Henry VII with Greyhound and Dragon supporters in another version.

Plate 4   The elaborate fan-vaulting in King's College Chapel,
          one of the great triumphs of early Tudor architecture.

valley from the north Wales coast. Faced with large Yorkist forces ably directed, Harlech at last surrendered on 14 August 1468.

William Herbert was now rewarded with the formal grant of Jasper Tudor's earldom of Pembroke on 8 September 1468. Herbert also secured the lordship of Gower during that year, a title that was confirmed by Edward IV the following May. Herbert had long enjoyed the custody of Gower, but the formal transfer of the honour by the fourth (and last) Mowbray Duke of Norfolk made the new Earl of Pembroke's position seem unassailable in Wales and the Marches.

The poet Lewis Glyn Cothi, a former Lancastrian, described Herbert, probably his new patron, as Edward IV's 'master-lock'. Guto'r Glyn, a steady Yorkist from Glyn Ceiriog (near Llangollen), was even more enthusiastic about the new Son of Prophecy.

According to H. T. Evans, 'in the whole of fifteenth century Welsh literature there is no more fervent longing for leadership, unity, and patriotism' than in the *cywydd* written by Guto'r Glyn to William Herbert after the fall of Harlech:

> Tax not Anglesey beyond what it can bear. Let not the Saxon rule in Gwynedd and Flint. Confer no offices on the descendants of Horsa. Appoint as constables of castles throughout Wales men of thine own nation. Make Glamorgan and Gwynedd, from Conway to Neath, a united whole. And should England resent it, Wales will rally to thy side.[6]

Banbury and Herbert's Death

William Herbert was to hold Pembroke and Gower for less than a year. Edward IV's encouragement of Herbert's ambition for his own reasons was one of the major factors in Warwick's loss of influence at court. The kingmaker's determination not to accept a secondary role now led to a renewal of the civil war in which Herbert was killed. As a result of this schism amongst the Yorkist leaders, there was a fleeting restoration of Lancastrian fortunes which ended in the death of Henry VI and his heir. Henry Tudor's life thus took an entirely new direction.

The genesis of these events lay in Warwick's conspiracy against

Edward IV which probably dated back to 1468. The King's younger brother, George, Duke of Clarence, was enlisted and Warwick arranged for Clarence to marry his own elder daughter, Isabel Neville. Initially, Warwick planned to seize Edward IV's person and rule in his name as York had done with Henry VI after the Battle of St Albans in 1455, and Warwick had done with the same king after the Battle of Northampton in 1460. Warwick may also have envisaged replacing Edward IV with Clarence as puppet king, as it was only in late 1470 that Edward's queen, Elizabeth Woodville, gave birth to a son and heir.

Warwick's plans came to fruition in July 1469 with a series of uprisings in the north of England in which popular discontent was directed against the King. Clarence had meanwhile married Isabel Neville at Calais on 11 July 1469. As rebel forces under 'Robin of Redesdale' marched southwards, Warwick landed in Kent and soon entered London. Edward IV now summoned to his aid two of his most loyal lieutenants, William Herbert, Earl of Pembroke, and Humphrey Stafford, the newly created Earl of Devon.

Herbert, at the head of a strong force of Welsh gentry and their followers, marched to Gloucester and then through the Cotswold Hills, heading for Northampton. Besides forces from Pembroke, Herbert's army included representatives of the veteran Yorkist family, the Dwnns of Kidwelly. In particular the Herbert and Vaughan clans from Brecon and the southern Marches were prominent in this largely Welsh army. But portents for the coming battle were not good. Although Herbert was joined by Devon's force from the West Country, a quarrel between the two leaders over billeting arrangements in Banbury immediately preceding the coming battle precluded effective coordination.

The two contesting forces, royalist and insurgent, the latter loyal to Warwick, met five miles north-east of Banbury at Edgecote on 26 July. Devon's forces were apparently never properly engaged. After a hard-fought day, the arrival of a small force of Warwick's supporters on the field led to the fatal assumption by Herbert's men that a new insurgent army had arrived. At this stage the Welshmen broke. William Herbert and his brother Richard were taken to Northampton and executed the following day on Warwick's orders.

Another leading Yorkist slain at Edgecote was Sir Thomas ap Roger Vaughan of Hergest, near Kington, in the Lordship of Huntington. He was taken home for burial in Kington Church, where his imposing alabaster tomb, which still survives, was said by the poet Lewis Glyn Cothi to have cost as much 'as a distant conquest'.

The defeat at Banbury was regarded in Wales as a national, rather than a dynastic, catastrophe. Lewis Glyn Cothi considered that 'the greatest of battles was lost by treachery; at Banbury dire vengeance fell upon Wales'. Guto'r Glyn wrote that 'My nation is destroyed, now that the earl is slain.'[7]

The destruction of Herbert, perhaps Edward IV's ablest military adviser, put the King in a hazardous position. Within a few days of Edgecote, Edward was captured by Warwick and eventually despatched to Middleham Castle in Yorkshire as a prisoner.

Yet Warwick was unable to rule effectively with Edward under duress. The King was thus released in October 1469 and began to work for a restoration of his influence. In west Wales, John Dwnn was appointed constable of Haverfordwest and steward of Llanstephan and Cilgerran Castles. Evidently this development alarmed local Lancastrians, for two of the grandsons of Gruffydd ap Nicholas, Morgan and Henry ap Thomas, seized Carmarthen Castle. The King's younger brother, Richard, Duke of Gloucester, was sent to the region to curb this latest upsurge of violence.

During February 1470 a rising in Lincolnshire, in which Warwick was implicated, posed yet another threat to Edward's rule. The King quickly crushed the rebels near Stamford on 12 March 1470, and later publicly named Warwick and Clarence as traitors. Warwick and other insurgent leaders now fled to Exeter, pursued by the King. From Devon, Warwick and Clarence sailed to Calais, but were refused entrance and finally found refuge with Louis XI of France. Once again, Edward IV seemed in the ascendant.

Lancastrian Restoration, 1470–1

Warwick now committed himself to an astonishing reversal of policy. Under the sponsorship of Louis XI, Henry VI's wife, Queen Margaret of Anjou, the most committed Lancastrian, was persuaded to accept Warwick as an ally in a new attempt to destroy Edward IV. Warwick, for his part, swore allegiance to Margaret, her heir Prince Edward and the House of Lancaster.

It was agreed that with French assistance Warwick and Clarence would land in England, eliminate Edward IV and restore Henry VI as rightful King. Margaret and her son, Prince Edward, would follow. Furthermore, it was agreed that Prince Edward would marry Warwick's young daughter, Anne Neville. Warwick was thus to be father of the next Lancastrian queen, and father-in-law of the Lancastrian heir. This was the political basis of the strange alliance between Queen Margaret and her erstwhile Lancastrian enemies. All now depended on whether Edward IV could be overcome by force of arms.

Warwick's strategy initially succeeded. Following the landing of his forces during September 1470 at Dartmouth and Plymouth in Devon, Edward IV's rule in effect collapsed. Along with a few associates, including Richard, Duke of Gloucester, Edward managed to reach King's Lynn in Norfolk. From here he sailed for Holland on 2 October 1470. In London, Henry VI was extracted from the Tower and nominally restored to the throne, a 'Readeption' that was to last from 3 October 1470 to 11 April 1471.

With Warwick in London controlling the restored Lancastrian government, Jasper Tudor returned to Pembroke Castle. Here he found his nephew, Henry Tudor, who according to Polydore Vergil, was 'kept as a prisoner, but honourably brought up with the wife of William Herbert'. Polydore also relates that Jasper took Henry to London where Henry VI gazed upon the fourteen-year-old boy and prophesied that he would heal the breach between the warring factions. Henry may indeed have been taken to London in the circumstances described, but Henry VI's prophecy seems too much like a later Tudor anecdote to be fully credible.[8]

However, whether true or not, the story of the meeting between Henry VI and Henry Tudor emerges as a striking Shakespearian passage underlining the later Tudor claim to the throne:

KING HENRY: My Lord of Somerset, what youth is that of whom you seem to have so tender care?
SOMERSET: My liege, it is young Henry, Earl of Richmond.
KING HENRY: Come hither, England's hope (*Lays his hand on his head*)

If secret powers
Suggest but truth to my divining thoughts,
This pretty lad will prove our country's bliss.
His looks are full of peaceful majesty,
His head by nature fram'd to wear a crown,
His hand to wield a sceptre, and himself,
Likely in time to bless a regal throne . . .

(*Henry VI*, Part III)

The Lancastrian restoration was short-lived. Louis XI had insisted that England should declare war on Burgundy as a price for his assistance to Warwick and Queen Margaret. Following the promised English declaration of war in February 1471, Duke Charles of Burgundy naturally gave Edward IV important backing in the form of ships, men and money. Edward's expedition to regain the throne set sail from Flushing on 11 March 1471, eventually landing at Ravenspur in the Humber estuary. An attempt to enter England at Cromer in East Anglia was abandoned because of local Lancastrian supporters.

From Yorkshire, Edward moved southwards with great speed while Warwick remained passively at Coventry. Clarence, meanwhile, abandoned Warwick and realigned himself with his brother, Edward IV. Marching directly to London, which he entered on 11 April 1471, the King was reunited with his wife. His infant son, Edward of Westminster, had been born in the sanctuary of the Abbey during the previous October following his flight to Holland. Fortified with the resources of London, a natural Yorkist constituency, Edward turned north and destroyed Warwick's army at Barnet on 14 April, a battle in which the King's arch-rebel was killed. Warwick the Kingmaker was thus finally removed from the gyrations of English politics.

That same day, 14 April, Queen Margaret landed at Weymouth in Dorset. The Lancastrian strategy was to march north, cross the Severn and link up with Welsh Lancastrian forces arrayed by Jasper Tudor. But the vital Severn crossing at Gloucester was denied to the main Lancastrian army. In an impressive forced march, Edward IV outpaced his enemies and brought them to battle at Tewkesbury on 4 May 1471. The Lancastrian heir, Prince Edward, was killed in the fighting, and many other Lancastrian nobles, including Edmund Beaufort II, Duke of Somerset, executed after the battle. Queen Margaret, captured by the victorious Yorkists, was later ransomed to Louis XI, and relegated to obscurity.

Edward IV returned to London on 21 May; that night Henry VI was put to death in the Tower, probably on Edward's orders. The direct line of the House of Lancaster was now extinct. Edward's position was unchallenged.

The Flight from Tenby

Despite the Lancastrian catastrophe at Tewkesbury, Jasper Tudor once again eluded his pursuers. He had advanced from Pembroke to Chepstow when the news of the Lancastrian defeat reached him. Edward IV now commissioned the veteran Yorkist, Sir Roger Vaughan of Tretower, to take Jasper. But it was Vaughan who was captured and summarily executed at Chepstow on Jasper's orders.

In view of the Yorkist victory at Tewkesbury, there was now no alternative for Jasper but to leave Wales with his nephew Henry Tudor, whom he had discovered in the Herbert household at Raglan Castle. Henry, through his mother's descent from John of Gaunt, was the residuary Lancastrian claimant to the throne. Jasper evidently decided that his nephew must be preserved from Edward IV's custody.

From Chepstow, Jasper thus retreated to Pembroke Castle where he was briefly besieged by a Yorkist force. The siege was lifted after eight days, and Jasper was able to escape with the fourteen-year-old Henry Tudor to Tenby.

Here the Mayor, Thomas White, provided assistance and a ship was made ready. On 2 June 1471 the two Lancastrian earls, Jasper and Henry Tudor, sailed in a barque from Tenby harbour for France.[9] Bad weather made them change their course and instead they landed at Le Conquet in Brittany. Soon they were given asylum by Duke Francis II. Henry Tudor was now to remain in exile for fourteen years before he was to set foot again in Wales at Mill Bay in August 1485.

6

Henry Tudor's Exile

Once in Brittany, Jasper and Henry Tudor were received by Duke Francis and allowed to remain in his virtually independent Duchy. There can be little doubt that Edward IV was concerned over the escape of Jasper and Henry from Tenby. According to Polydore Vergil, Edward took 'very grievously' the news of their friendly reception by Duke Francis. The English King at some stage offered a substantial reward for the two fugitives, but the Duke stuck by his promise. Apparently Jasper and Henry were separated and guarded carefully so that no threat could be posed to Edward IV.

It soon transpired that the bad weather which forced Jasper and Henry to make their landfall in Brittany rather than France was providential. Jasper had no doubt believed that as Louis XI was instrumental in providing the assistance which had resulted in the brief Lancastrian restoration of 1470–1, he and Henry would be welcome in France. But the support given by Louis XI to the strange alliance between Warwick and Queen Margaret had been primarily a matter of statecraft. Accordingly, when relations between England and France, after a brief outbreak of hostilities, were regularized by the Treaty of Picquigny in August 1475, it appears probable that Louis would have handed over the fugitives had they been in his custody.

Following the Treaty of Picquigny which improved English relations with France and consequently the English bargaining position with Brittany, Edward IV made fresh attempts to obtain Henry Tudor. Through his emissaries, Edward apparently succeeded in persuading Duke Francis of Brittany that all he wished was to arrange an appropriate marriage for Henry Tudor, perhaps to one of his daughters, so that the dynastic problem could be solved.

Henry Tudor was therefore sent with the English representatives to St Malo for repatriation. In great 'agony of mind' (Polydore Vergil), he himself believed that he was going to his death. At this juncture, one of Duke Francis's advisers persuaded him that Henry Tudor's fate would probably be quite other than that outlined by Edward IV's emissaries. Peter Landois, the Breton treasurer, was therefore dispatched to St Malo, and through a ruse rescued Henry Tudor from the English officials. Duke Francis, however, renewed his assurances that Henry would remain guarded, the assurances were kept, and apparently for the rest of his reign Edward IV made no serious attempt to retrieve Henry Tudor.

Yorkist Rule Consolidated

There were good reasons why Edward IV should feel increasingly secure. After the decisive Yorkist military victories in 1471, a large proportion of the estates of Warwick and the defeated Lancastrian leaders had been confiscated by the crown. Former prominent followers of Henry VI, such as Sir John Fortescue and the cleric John Morton, had made their peace with Edward. French hostility had been partly responsible for Edward's temporary overthrow in 1470, but as we have seen, a rapprochement with France had been negotiated with the Treaty of Picquigny in 1475.

In Wales, too, the Yorkist regime was beginning to bring increased stability although the underlying tensions remained. Warwick's lordship of Glamorgan had passed to the crown in 1471, and was later assigned to Richard, Duke of Gloucester, the King's younger brother. In 1479 Edward IV persuaded the young William Herbert, the son and heir of Edward's champion who had been executed after Banbury, to exchange the earldom of Pembroke for the earldom of Huntingdon. Pembroke was then granted to Edward, Prince of Wales.

The King also acquired from Herbert the lordship of Gower, which was now regarded as part of the Mowbray estates and vested in the King's young second son, Richard, as husband (and later widower) of the Mowbray heiress. Thus the crown possessed under differing titles the Royal Principality, the Duchy of Lancaster estates, the earldom of March and the three most important lordships in south Wales, Glamorgan, Gower and Pembroke. Of the great Marcher lords, only Henry, Duke of Buckingham, Lord of Brecon, remained.

This concentration of royal power was augmented by constitutional innovation in Wales. During his first reign, 1461–9, Edward IV had pursued his objectives in Wales through using the talents, civil and military, of William Herbert, first Earl of Pembroke. But such a policy of using the Herbert family was not possible after the Yorkist Restoration of 1471, due to the youth and inexperience of Herbert's son, William Herbert II (1455–90).

Instead, a council was established for Edward IV's heir, Edward of Westminister, who was created Prince of Wales at the age of about eight months in June 1471. This council, set up the following month, was gradually given increased status and power over the Royal Principality in the task of controlling and rationalizing crown administration in Wales and relations with the remaining Marcher lords. To this end, Edward IV himself met with the Marcher lords at Shrewsbury in June 1473, concluding agreements and indentures for preserving law and order which the King signed as Earl of March – the greatest Marcher lord – and not as the Sovereign.

A further conference at Ludlow in March 1476 between the Prince's council and the Marcher lords extended the influence of the council from the Royal Principality into the March. Later that year, authority was given for the council to array men to deal with disorder in the area of its jurisdiction, including the English border counties, and in 1478 ordinances were issued for the protection of the peace in Shrewsbury. Gradually, the direct influence of the crown, through the council at Ludlow, was being extended over the whole of Wales and the Marches.[1]

The growing acceptance of Yorkist rule and the continuing prosperity which accompanied it, was not merely the result of Edward IV's relatively efficient government. There was also the stabilizing factor that Henry Tudor, an unknown exile, did not seem a credible candidate for the throne. On strict legitimist grounds, the Yorkist line seemed to have the better claim. As we have seen, Edward IV's father, Richard, Duke of York, was descended, through his mother, from the second son of Edward III.

Henry's claim to the crown was considered inadequate as it came from his mother, Margaret Beaufort. The Beauforts, who were named after a Duchy of Lancaster castle in north-east France, had been born the bastard children of John of Gaunt (1340–99), Duke of Lancaster, by his mistress, Katherine Swynford. The extensive holdings of the Duchy of Lancaster, it should be noted, had come to John of Gaunt through his first marriage to the Lancastrian heiress, Blanche. Their son was Henry of Lancaster, or Henry IV, the founder of the main Lancastrian line with his deposition of Richard II in 1399.

During Richard II's reign, the Beauforts had been legitimized by Act of Parliament in 1397. But Henry IV had added a caveat, *Excepta Dignitate Regali*, 'The Royal Dignity Excepted', when this Act of Legitimization had been confirmed by one of Henry's early Parliaments.

It was moot whether Henry IV's rider was valid as it had been given no Parliamentary sanction. But doubt continued to remain over any Beaufort claim to the throne. Nevertheless, the main line of Lancaster had been extinguished in 1471, and hence Henry Tudor became the residual Lancastrian candidate. But Henry Tudor was careful not to make any direct claim to the crown on legitimist grounds during Edward IV's reign. He remained of course the Lancastrian Earl of Richmond.

Following Henry's victory at Bosworth Field, the first Parliament of his reign merely enacted that the crown was now vested in his person. Henry himself in an address to the Commons following the Act of Accession in November 1485 claimed a legitimate hereditary title. But he was also careful to stress that he held the throne by 'the true judgement of God', *verum dei judicium*, a form of divine right sanctified by the God of Battles – or the right of conquest – at Bosworth.

These reservations over Henry's Lancastrian descent explain the symbolism of the greyhound in early Tudor heraldry. The greyhound was a favourite badge of the Lancastrian monarchs, and when King Henry VI made his half-brother, Edmund Tudor, Earl of Richmond he assigned to him the royal greyhound as a supporter of his arms. Henry Tudor clearly attached great significance to the armorial greyhound which he inherited from his father, for it both symbolized and strengthened his links with the main house of Lancaster. Hence the greyhound of Richmond as well as the Welsh dragon stood as a supporter in Henry VII's arms. But Henry also prominently displayed the badge of the Beaufort portcullis to symbolize his mother's branch of the Lancastrian family.

During the later years of Henry Tudor's exile in Brittany and

France, these considerations still lay in the future. It was the extraordinary events of 1483 that completely changed Henry's prospects. The early, premature death of Edward IV, the disappearance of the Yorkist heir, Edward V, and his younger brother Duke Richard, and the usurpation of Richard III transformed Henry Tudor's status. From an insecure exile, he now became a serious claimant for the throne of England.

Richard III's Usurpation

After a brief illness, perhaps typhoid, Edward IV died at the age of forty on 9 April 1483. His heir was his twelve-year-old son, Edward of Westminster, Prince of Wales, who now became Edward V. Next in succession was Edward's younger brother, the ten-year-old Richard, Duke of York.

During the later years of Edward IV's reign, the King's younger brother, Richard, Duke of Gloucester (b. 1452) had become indispensable. Richard was Edward IV's sole surviving brother. Edmund, Duke of Rutland had been killed at Wakefield in 1460, while George, Duke of Clarence, 'false, fleeting, perjur'd Clarence', had been put to death on Edward IV's orders in 1478 after his parliamentary attainder for 'unnatural and loathly treason'. The legend that Clarence was drowned in a malmsey-butt is probably true.

Gloucester was married to Anne Neville, the younger daughter of Warwick the Kingmaker, and he had succeeded to many of Warwick's estates north of the River Trent. Richard had also furthered the interests of the city of York, his northern 'capital', during Edward IV's reign and thus his position in the north was particularly strong. In the Scottish war of 1482, Gloucester had recovered Berwick, which had been traded to the Scots by Queen Margaret after the Battle of Towton in 1461.

Edward IV had first appointed Richard Warden of the west Marches towards Scotland in 1470. The Commission had been renewed in 1471 (after the final destruction of the Lancastrian dynasty) and in 1480. Richard's influence had soon become paramount in the north and his many residences between 1471 and 1483 included the strongholds of

Sheriff Hutton (near York), Middleham, Sandal, Penrith and Carlisle. In January 1483, after the recovery of Berwick from the Scots, Edward IV created for his brother an impressive hereditary palatine lordship composed of the counties of Cumberland and Westmorland. In effect, the King's writ would no longer run in the palatine now given to Gloucester.

With the death of Edward IV in April 1483, Duke Richard was thus the leader of what his recent biographer, Charles Ross, has described as 'an exceptionally large and powerful northern affinity'. It was this power-base that underwrote Richard's bid for the throne in 1483.

Despite this political muscle, on the death of Edward IV Duke Richard probably felt threatened by the powerful Woodville family, the relatives of Edward's Queen Elizabeth. The Woodvilles had been hostile to Clarence and with his elimination in 1478 their influence had increased at court. They had also acquired the custody of the Yorkist heir, Edward, Prince of Wales, and his young brother, Richard, Duke of York.

Richard of Gloucester was the obvious candidate for the Protectorship during Edward V's minority. But the Woodvilles were also in a strong (yet not dominant) position in the Royal Council which assumed executive powers following Edward IV's death. Richard may well have calculated that the Woodvilles' control of Edward V, combined with their other assets, was a serious challenge to his own position, a challenge that could prove mortal in the ruthless world of fifteenth-century politics. This situation was now to lead to a virtual resurgence of civil war and to the eventual destruction of the Yorkist dynasty.

Gloucester may not originally have decided to usurp the throne. But whatever his precise motives, which have been debated ever since, in order to seize effective power in the realm he had to move with great speed, and with great violence. He was in the north when Edward IV died, while Edward, Prince of Wales was in Ludlow, with Anthony Woodville, Earl Rivers, the Queen's brother, in attendance. In London the council was divided between the factions of William, Lord Hastings and the Woodvilles. Hastings had been a boon companion of Edward IV, was loyal to his memory and advocated giving Richard full powers as Protector; the Woodvilles wanted the Protector only to be the chief member of the council. Hastings now warned Richard of the potential threat from the Woodvilles and urged him to enter London with security forces of his own.

Edward V and Rivers had left Ludlow on about 24 April 1483, while Richard was moving southwards towards London from York. At this stage Henry Stafford, Duke of Buckingham, the last great independent magnate in the Welsh March, sent an emissary to Richard assuring him of his support. Buckingham then joined Richard at Northampton on 29 April. The two Dukes quickly concerted their plans and it was later believed that Richard 'even then discovered to Henry his intent of usurping the Kingship' (Polydore Vergil).

Following his arrival at Stony Stratford on 28 April Rivers rode back to Northampton to greet Richard of Gloucester. After a pleasant dinner on 29 April with all suspicions lulled, Rivers was suddenly arrested at dawn the next day. Richard's forces then intercepted the young King's party at Stony Stratford and took possession of Edward V. The King's half-brother, Lord Richard Grey, a son of the Dowager Queen by her first husband, was arrested as was Sir Thomas Vaughan, Edward V's chamberlain. The royal escort was dismissed. Rivers, Grey and Vaughan were then despatched to Pontefract Castle. Here they were summarily executed on 25 June, almost certainly on Richard's orders.

On 4 May, Edward V entered London, only to be despatched to the Tower. Preparations for his coronation went ahead as planned. Soon Richard was given full powers as Protector by the council. He was also made the guardian of the King's person. Lord Hastings, however, remained loyal to Edward V and the true Yorkist line, and evidently opposed any usurpation of the crown. He was suddenly arrested at a council meeting on 13 June, accused of treason by Richard and summarily beheaded outside the Tower. Archbishop Rotherham and Bishop John Morton of Ely, both members of the council whom Richard considered unreliable, were confined; Morton was sent to Buckingham's seat at Brecon Castle.

Richard's plans were almost complete. The Dowager Queen Elizabeth was persuaded to let the young Richard, Duke of York, out of her custody in sanctuary at Westminster Abbey. He disappeared into the Tower to join his brother, Edward V; neither of Edward IV's sons was seen alive again outside.

In this way, the stage was now set for the final usurpation of the crown. On 22 June 1483 Dr Ralph Shaw, a prominent theologian, preached a sermon at St Paul's Cross advocating that the Protector should be King. The grounds given were that Edward IV's two children were bastards because of an alleged pre-marriage contract by the Yorkist King. Richard and Buckingham were present at the sermon. Others of Richard's propagandists in the pulpits of London stated that Edward IV himself was also illegitimate. Meanwhile, large contingents of Richard's northern troops assembled outside London.

Richard's claim was again advanced to the mayor and aldermen of London, meeting in the Guildhall, by Duke Henry of Buckingham on 24 June. The following day, an assembly of lords and other notables was also addressed by Buckingham; the assembly drew up a petition asking Richard to assume the throne. On 26 June the assembly met again and presented the petition to Richard at his mother's London house, Baynard's Castle. The Protector then went to Westminster Hall where he took his seat on the King's Bench, so indicating his formal assumption of the throne. The reign of Richard III thus began officially on that day, 26 June 1483.[2]

Finally, when even more of Richard's forces had entered London, a coronation of great splendour, originally planned for Edward V, was staged on 6 July 1483. Soon after, Richard III, accompanied by Buckingham, left on a royal progress westwards. At Gloucester the two men parted, Buckingham proceeding to Brecon.

According to Sir Thomas More's famous account, *The History of Richard III*, it was shortly afterwards, probably in August when Richard had repaired to Warwick, that the new King gave orders for the murder of Edward IV's two sons in the Tower. The disappearance of the two Princes was now to initiate the events that led directly to Bosworth Field.

Buckingham's Revolt

Within three months of Richard's usurpation, there was already a significant movement in London and parts of southern England to remove the Princes in the Tower from royal custody. Soon the conviction grew that Richard III was responsible for their death, a conviction shared by most historians ever since. The movement against Richard now developed into a plot to replace him by Henry

Tudor who would then marry Elizabeth of York, Edward IV's eldest daughter. The dynastic claims of both Lancaster and York would then be satisfied.

The conspiracy was probably initiated by Lady Margaret Beaufort, Henry Tudor's mother, and the wife of Thomas, Lord Stanley. According to Polydore Vergil, the plot was supported from the beginning by Edward IV's dowager queen, Elizabeth Woodville. It seemed obvious then and later that her support for the conspiracy against Richard III indicated her belief that her sons were already dead. For there could be little hope for a movement to put Henry Tudor on the throne unless dissident Yorkists believed that there was no hope of restoring either of the sons of Edward IV. From the beginning, therefore, the conspiracy to replace Richard III was supported by some Yorkists as well as those who remained loyal to Lancaster.

According to Polydore Vergil, after the presumed death of the Princes in the Tower Margaret Beaufort saw an entirely new prospect for her son, whom she had not seen since his flight to Brittany in 1471. Margaret then confided in her Welsh-born physician, Lewis, and sent him with her plan to Queen Elizabeth in sanctuary at Westminster Abbey. It was then that an understanding was probably reached by which the Woodville affinity would support Henry Tudor as a serious claimant to the crown if he would undertake to marry the Queen's eldest daughter, Elizabeth of York, or if she were dead, Edward IV's younger daughter, Cicely.

Margaret Beaufort's steward, Reginald Bray, now became her confidential agent in the development of the initial stages of the conspiracy. At the same time, Queen Elizabeth brought into the plot Thomas, Marquis of Dorset, her eldest son by her first marriage, and Peter Courtenay, Bishop of Exeter and his brother, Edward, heir to the earldom of Devon.

As the conspiracy against Richard grew, Margaret Beaufort arranged for a reliable priest, Christopher Urswick, to go to Brittany to inform Henry Tudor of developments. But alternative arrangements had to be made when Margaret Beaufort and Queen Elizabeth learnt that Henry Stafford, second Duke of Buckingham, was also advocating the replacement of Richard III by Henry Tudor. This gave the conspiracy added backing which was now to result in a major, but badly coordinated, rising against the King during October 1483.

Buckingham's precise motives in rebelling against Richard III remain something of a mystery. But what seems clear is that as the conspiracy grew, so the centre of activity moved to Brecon Castle, Buckingham's chief seat in Wales. Here Bishop John Morton of Ely had been sent for internment by a rightly suspicious Richard III.

Henry Stafford, Duke of Buckingham, was the holder of great estates in England and in the Welsh March, where he was Lord of Brecon, Hay, Huntington, Newport and Caus, near Shrewsbury. On his father's side, Buckingham was descended from Anne, daughter of Thomas of Woodstock, fifth son of Edward III. His grandfather, the first Duke of Buckingham, was killed at the Battle of Northampton in 1460, fighting for the Lancastrian cause. Buckingham had been married to a Woodville, but against his wishes, and he disliked the family as upstarts.

Buckingham's mother was a daughter of Edmund Beaufort I, Duke of Somerset, the leading Lancastrian, who had also been killed at St Albans in 1455. Moreover, Buckingham's uncle, Henry Stafford, was Margaret Beaufort's second husband until his death in 1471. Buckingham was therefore not only an overmighty subject, but he was close to the throne by birth, and intimately connected with the Lancastrian cause. His deviation in initially supporting Richard III's usurpation was now to have fatal consequences.

Indispensable to Richard of Gloucester during the planning of his usurpation, Buckingham had been extravagantly rewarded. In May 1483 he had been made justice and chamberlain of north and south Wales and given custody of all royal castles in Wales from the Severn to the Dee, including those of the Duchy of Lancaster and the Mortimer earldom of March.

By confirming these grants after his usurpation, Richard III had cast away all the concentration of royal authority in Wales which had been won by Edward IV. Buckingham's extraordinary authority in Wales may thus have predisposed him towards rebellion as much as his Lancastrian antecedents and the disappearance of Edward IV's children in the summer of 1483.

Buckingham, as we have seen, had accompanied Richard III on his post-coronation progress as far as Gloucester. But once he had returned to Brecon, Buckingham's loyalty to Richard had begun to lapse. It remains uncertain whether Buckingham had originally intended to take Richard III's place himself, or whether he had from the beginning envisaged Henry Tudor as Richard's successor, as recorded by Polydore Vergil.

It also remains possible that Bishop John Morton may have suggested Henry Tudor as a claimant to the throne. Another element in the origins of Buckingham's revolt may lie in the fact that his personal relations with Richard had quickly deteriorated, and that Richard had been tardy in conveying to him some disputed Bohun lands in Herefordshire. But whatever his precise motives, Buckingham was won over to Lady Margaret Beaufort's conspiracy against Richard by September 1483.

During this month, probably around the 24th, Buckingham wrote to Henry Tudor in Brittany informing him that a rising at differing centres in southern England would take place during October, and asking Henry to launch an expedition. The later Acts of Attainder against the more prominent rebels stated that 18 October had been arranged for the outbreak of the rebellion.

Bishop Morton now took an increasingly prominent part in the preparations and further messages passed between Brecon, London and Brittany. Unfortunately for the conspirators, Richard III learnt of the projected rising and was able to make his dispositions accordingly. John, Lord Howard, created Duke of Norfolk by Richard, was entrusted with the defence of London, while the King decided to concentrate on the defeat of Buckingham.

During mid-October, Richard III moved from London to Lincoln to Leicester, issuing letters and commissions for security forces to be mobilized in the south and west of England. In the Welsh Marches, the Vaughans of Tretower were alerted, together with their kinsfolk. This powerful clan were enemies of the Tudor cause; it will be remembered that at Chepstow in 1471 Jasper Tudor had ordered the execution of Sir Roger Vaughan of Tretower.

Buckingham had widely overestimated his chances of success. As Richard III moved southwards from Leicester, Buckingham made his move by advancing north-eastwards from Brecon towards the Severn crossings. Evidently he hoped to cross the river south of Worcester and join with the other insurgents in the West Country. Meanwhile, on 18 October there were simultaneous risings in Maidstone, Rochester and Gravesend in the south-east, and in Newbury (Berkshire), Salisbury and Exeter, where Henry Tudor was proclaimed King by the Bishop, Sir Peter Courtenay.

While Buckingham was delayed by exceptionally bad autumn weather at Weobley in west Herefordshire, the home of Lord Ferrers, Sir Thomas Vaughan of Tretower and his brothers sacked Brecon Castle, thus eliminating Buckingham's main base. Floods swept away many bridges and made it generally impossible for Buckingham to continue his advance.

Moreover, although Buckingham's authority in Wales seemed impressive, he could not appeal to Welsh national sentiment. At the first sign of trouble he was abandoned by his conscripted Welsh levies, 'whom he as a sore and hard-dealing man had brought to the field against their wills and without any lust to fight for him, rather by rigorous commandment than for money' (Polydore Vergil). With all bridges and passes into England guarded, Buckingham went into hiding. Betrayed, he was brought to Salisbury, where the King was found, and executed there on 2 November. Richard refused to see his erstwhile ally prior to his execution.

By this time, the rebellion in general had fizzled out. The Courtenays had retreated from Exeter, which Richard had occupied on 12 November, into Cornwall, where Henry was again proclaimed King at Bodmin. From Cornwall, Henry's West Country supporters fled to the Continent.

Meanwhile Henry had sailed in mid-October with about fifteen ships from Brittany. Making landfall at either Plymouth or Poole in Dorset, after severe storms had forced back some of his vessels, Henry refused to be trapped by some of Richard III's soldiers who tried to persuade him to come ashore. Instead he set sail for France, landing in Normandy. From there he marched with his followers to Brittany, where he learnt for the first time that Buckingham was dead. Henry Tudor's first expedition to gain the crown had ended in failure.

Henry's Escape to France

Despite Richard III's impressive success in crushing Buckingham's revolt, Henry of Richmond's position was greatly strengthened by the events of late 1483. A group of distinguished exiles, both Lancastrians and dissident Yorkists, now made their way to join Henry and Jasper Tudor in Brittany and soon began to appear as an alternative government. These refugees included Peter Courtenay, Bishop of Exeter, Thomas Grey, Marquis of Dorset, the Dowager Queen's eldest son by her first husband, and Sir Edward Woodville, the Dowager Queen's brother. Bishop John Morton, who as we have seen played a central role in Buckingham's revolt, fled to Flanders, and he too may have made his way to Brittany.

Initially the fugitives from Richard III congregated at Vannes. They then joined Henry at Rennes and in the cathedral there on Christmas Day 1483 they reaffirmed their allegiance to Henry 'by plighting of their troths and solemn covenants' (Polydore Vergil). For his part, Henry Tudor swore that once he became King he would marry Elizabeth of York, Edward IV's eldest daughter. His supporters then swore homage to him 'as though he already had been created king'.

Henry also retained the sympathy of many adherents in England despite Richard III's extensive Bills of Attainder presented to Parliament during the first months of 1484. A number of Henry Tudor's supporters had already been executed in the aftermath of Buckingham's revolt. The mainspring of the conspiracy in 1483, Lady Margaret Beaufort, escaped the penalties of attainder. But her titles and her estates were forfeited, the latter given to her husband, Thomas, Lord Stanley.

Richard's lenient action in this case was no doubt intended to enlist the loyalty of Lord Stanley, of whom he was rightly suspicious. But there can be little doubt that Richard III's power-base was dangerously slender, relying at the outset of his reign on four overmighty subjects – Buckingham, Lord Stanley, Henry Percy, fourth Earl of Northumberland and John, Lord Howard, whom he created Duke of Norfolk. Buckingham's elimination narrowed this base even further, and events were to show that in the final test only Norfolk could be relied upon.

Richard also attempted to gain the support of the gentry by the extensive use of his powers of patronage. Many of the Welsh gentry were given annuities and other royal perquisites; Rhys ap Thomas, for example, was given an annuity of forty marks. But the violent events of Richard's usurpation, and above all the disappearance of Edward IV's sons, meant that his reign lacked general acceptance. In Wales, national sentiment united both Lancastrian and dissident Yorkist sympathies behind the cause of Henry Tudor.

Richard made strenuous attempts in a number of directions to forestall Henry Tudor's next attempt on the throne. Before the Parliament of 1484 was over, the King required the lords spiritual and temporal to take an oath of loyalty to his son, Prince Edward. This oath was to become effective in the event of Richard's removal, but this attempt to reinforce his dynasty was frustrated when the Prince died on 9 April 1484. Earlier, Richard had persuaded the Dowager Queen to leave the sanctuary of Westminster under safe-conduct. There was thus a threat that the Queen's daughter might not be available to marry Henry Tudor, should the circumstances envisaged at Rennes cathedral arise.

Later that year, Richard attempted to put pressure on Duke Francis of Brittany to surrender Henry Tudor. His efforts in this direction were facilitated by the illness of Duke Francis and the devolution of effective power to Peter Landois, the treasurer of the dukedom. Landois was persuaded by Richard's agents to surrender Henry. Providentially for Henry, Bishop John Morton in Flanders learnt of the plot and informed Christopher Urswick, Margaret Beaufort's agent. Urswick conveyed the intelligence to Henry, who was at Vannes.

By a stratagem, Henry managed to escape across the border into Anjou. Led by Jasper Tudor, the leading English exiles in Brittany also escaped as a group into France. Learning of Henry's flight, Landois sent troops to arrest him. They reached the French border a bare hour after their prey had left Brittany. Meanwhile, on 11 October 1484, the French Council of Regency ordered that Henry, as a valuable diplomatic pawn, should be given an honourable reception. Money was also made available. Duke Francis of Brittany now recovered his health, repudiated Landois' policy and arranged for the rest of Henry's supporters, about 300 men, to be sent into France.

Henry's future was now dependent on French policy towards Brittany and England. Following the death of Louis XI in August 1483, France was ruled by the minority administration of his son, Charles VIII, who had succeeded at the age of thirteen. The Council of Regency was in fact dominated by Anne of Beaujeu, Louis XI's eldest child. It was 'a cardinal objective of her policy to ensure that Brittany in due course should become part of the Kingdom of France. It followed that if

Henry Tudor could be used to contribute to that end, he would so be used.'[3]

Following his flight to France, Henry Tudor met Charles VIII and stated that he was the rightful claimant to the English throne. There was a suggestion of goodwill, but no concrete French support for the mounting of a second expedition at this stage. But Henry's cause was strengthened by the recruitment of John de la Vere, Earl of Oxford, a veteran Lancastrian military commander who escaped from Hammes Castle (near Calais). According to Polydore Vergil, Henry was 'ravished with joy' at Oxford's arrival and 'began to hope better of his affairs'.

The credibility of Henry's cause was further underlined when on 16 March 1485 Richard III's consort, Queen Anne, died. The King had thus no hope of consolidating a dynasty in the near future, and Richard's chief sanction against Henry of Richmond was now essentially a military one. The timing of Henry's forthcoming expedition remained dependent on French policy, but of its eventual coming there seemed little doubt. Accordingly, the final preparations for his reception were now put under way in both England and Wales during the early months of 1485.

Final Preparations

As early as 7 December 1484, Richard III had issued his first proclamation against Henry and Jasper Tudor and their allies. Henry Tudor was accused of taking the name and title of a royal estate to which he had no right, and the King's subjects were called upon to be arrayed if necessary. Both Owen Tudor and Lady Margaret Beaufort were declared illegitimate. The proclamation was repeated on 23 June 1485, barely six weeks before Henry sailed from the mouth of the Seine.

But according to Polydore Vergil, during these early months of 1485 Richard relaxed many of his defensive precautions on the assumption that Henry would be unable to organize sufficient support from the French court. Richard had therefore withdrawn his naval patrols from the Channel and stood down some garrisons. But 'lest he might be found altogether unready . . . he commanded nobles and gentlemen dwelling about the sea coast, and chiefly the Welshmen to keep watch . . . that his adversaries should not have ready recovery of the shore and come a land . . .' Accordingly an elaborate system of beacons was organized along the south coasts of England and Wales, and probably Milford Haven was closely watched by Richard's security forces.

There were particular defensive precautions in west Wales when in early 1484 Pembroke, Tenby and other fortresses were put into a state of readiness. These castles included Cilgerran which guarded access to Cardiganshire.[4]

Buckingham's revolt and the national appeal of Henry Tudor forced Richard III to readopt the earlier Yorkist policy of relying on the Herbert family in south Wales. William Herbert, Earl of Huntingdon was justice of south Wales at the time of Edward IV's death. He had been replaced by Buckingham prior to Richard's usurpation. But following Buckingham's execution Herbert had been reappointed justice of south Wales. He was also given some of Buckingham's castles in the region, including Brecon, and the stewardship of some Mortimer and Lancastrian estates in the southern March. Following the death of Herbert's first Woodville wife, his loyalty to Richard was further cemented when in February 1484 he was betrothed to Katherine Plantagenet, the King's bastard daughter.[5]

As a further security precaution Herbert's kinsmen, the Vaughans of Tretower, guarded the valleys of the Wye and the Usk in south-east Wales. Sir James Tyrell was placed in control of the upper valley of the Tywi through his command of the castles of Llandovery and Builth, so closing the route into the middle March taken by Jasper Tudor in 1461. The road which Henry Tudor eventually took in August 1485 from Dale to Shrewsbury was thus probably intended to avoid these defensive deployments by Richard III in south Wales. The concept of advancing to Shrewsbury was also strategically sound as it would enable Henry to make contact with the Stanleys, and pick up other support from the home ground of the Tudors in north Wales.

During the early months of 1485, Henry left Paris and went to Rouen and then to the mouth of the Seine to organize his expedition. Following the death of Queen Anne in March 1485, a rumour reached Henry that Richard III intended to marry Elizabeth of York. The news 'pinched Henry by the very stomach' (Polydore Vergil), because much of his support depended on his own projected marriage with Elizabeth.

Henry decided to reinsure himself by approaching Walter Herbert, 'a man of ancient authority amongst the Welshmen', who had a marriageable sister. Walter Herbert was the second son of Henry Tudor's former guardian, William Herbert, first Earl of Pembroke, and thus the brother of the Earl of Huntingdon, the justice of south Wales. Probably in this way Henry hoped to enlist further support from amongst the Welsh Yorkists.

Apparently the message does not seem to have reached Herbert. But a 'better messenger' came out of Wales with the news from John Morgan of Tredegar that Rhys ap Thomas, 'a man of great service and valiant', and John Savage of Cheshire were committed to Henry's cause, and that Reginald Bray, Margaret Beaufort's steward, had 'no small sum of money to pay soldiers wages'.

John Morgan (d. 1504) was later given a number of clerical preferments by Henry VII, and in 1496 was made Bishop of St Davids. His brother, Trahaiarn Morgan, a lawyer, was related to the Dwnns of Carmarthenshire, and owned land at Muddlescwm, near Kidwelly, consequently being known as Morgan of Kidwelly (not to be confused with Richard III's Attorney-General, Morgan Kidwelly, who was a Dorset man and no relation). Another relative of these two brothers, Evan Morgan, was active in Henry's cause, and is reported to have joined him in Brittany after the collapse of Buckingham's rebellion.

Henry had already sent messages, written in a semi-regal style, to his confederates in Wales warning them of his impending arrival. His alleged letter to John ap Meredith, an influential chieftain of Eifionydd in Gwynedd, north Wales, has been preserved:

By the King

Right trusty and well-beloved, we greet you well. And whereas it is so that, through the help of almighty God, the assistance of our loving and true subjects, and the great confidence we have in the nobles and commons of this our principality of Wales, we be entered into the same, purposing, by the help above rehearsed, in all haste possible to descend into our realm of England, not only for the adoption of the Crown, unto us of right apertaining, but also for the oppression of the tyrant, Richard late Duke of Gloucester, usurper of our said right; and moreover to reduce our said realm of

England into its ancient estate, and honour, and property and prosperity, as this our said principality of Wales and the people of the same to their erst liberties, delivering them of such miserable servitudes as they have long piteously long stood in: We desire and pray you, and upon your allegiance strictly charge and command you that, immediately upon the sight hereof with all such power as ye may make, defensibly arrayed for the war, ye address you towards us, wheresoever we shall be, to our aid

. . .

Given under our signet at our

. . .

To our Trusty and well-beloved John ap Meredith ap Ieuan ap Meredith.[6]

In the summer of 1485 the time for decision was at hand for Henry of Richmond. Thomas, Lord Stanley, his brother Sir William Stanley (justice of north Wales) and Gilbert Talbot had sent secret messages of support. Another supporter was William Griffifth of Penrhyn, grandson of Gwilym ap Gruffydd, and thus a distant kinsman of Henry Tudor's. French policy during the summer of 1485 was now concerned with a possible understanding between Richard III and Duke Francis of Brittany. So it was in the French interest to support Henry's expedition as a means of weakening Richard III.

His preparations concluded, Henry Tudor sailed from Harfleur at the mouth of the Seine on 1 August 1485. His force included Jasper Tudor and the loyal exiles who had sustained him in Brittany since Buckingham's abortive revolt. There was also a French contingent of some 2,000 men.

Henry Tudor's long exile was over. His landing had been carefully planned for Mill Bay, near Dale, at the northern entrance to Milford Haven, where maximum secrecy and surprise were possible. From nearby Haverfordwest, his route would lie along the Cardiganshire coast and through the Cambrian mountains into the upper valley of the Severn leading to Shrewsbury. Here, contact would have to be made with the Stanleys for the decisive confrontation with Richard III.

In this strategy, a swift advance to Shrewsbury was vital. Henry's preparations in Wales had been advanced by the longstanding sympathies of the bardic fraternity in general and by a particular understanding with Rhys ap Thomas, the most influential magnate in west Wales. Without the political preparation by the poets and the military assistance of Rhys ap Thomas, Henry Tudor's march through Wales in August 1485 would not have been possible.

7

Prophecy and Politics

The effective and enthusiastic support given by the Welsh poets to Henry Tudor in the period before his expedition of 1485 was the culmination of a very long tradition of prophetic poetry. Central to this prophetic (or vaticinatory) tradition was the projection of a national hero, perhaps from across the sea, who would one day lead the Welsh to victory. Then a British king would once again rule in London.

It was a compehensive, effective and even necessary tradition during the centuries of retreat before the Saxons and the Normans and the poets played an indispensable role in transferring these prophecies from generation to generation. The national hero, the 'Son of Prophecy' (*Mab Darogan*) was usually one of the legendary Welsh hero-kings of the Dark Ages, Owain, Cadwaladr or Arthur. The advent of the Son of Prophecy would initiate the battles and the bloodshed that would result in the final triumph of the Welsh and their Celtic allies. Then the golden age would be at hand.

Hope was thus inherent in the poetry of prophecy. No matter how great the vicissitudes of the present, it was implied that present circumstances could change, the Welsh cause might find new allies, and the tyrants would and could be overthrown. The poetry of prophecy thus had a powerful political content, as emerged during the rebellion of Owain Glyn Dŵr. Two generations later, prophecy and politics converged on another Son of Prophecy. This time Henry Tudor was victorious and the poets believed that the ancient prophecies had been fulfilled in his person.

The tradition of prophecy of which Henry Tudor was the ultimate incarnation was thus a very old one, and it drew on many eclectic sources. Some of its roots included the prophetic element in Christianity, as well as the story of the Sibylline oracles. It probably owed something to the popular divinations common in Britain during the middle ages, including the pseudo-science of astrology. The prophetic tradition was found in many European countries, and one of the most potent European legends in the middle ages was that of the German emperor, Barbarossa, who waited in his cave for the day of his triumphant return.

In Welsh literary history, the sixth-century poets Taliesin and Myrddin (Merlin) may be termed prophetic poets. Although none of the work of the latter has survived, the invocation of these poets by their successors demonstrates that the tradition of prophecy went back to the beginnings of recorded Welsh history. According to Sir Thomas Parry

> early in their history the prophetic poems developed out of simple predictions inspired by the patriotic zeal of the author into out-and-out prophecies, and the authors showed an increasing eagerness to give their work a supernatural colouring by bringing in significant details.[1]

In the first extant, specific poem of prophecy, the tenth-century *Armes Prydein* ('The Prophecy of Britain'), there is a call for a Celtic confederacy against the Saxons, who will be driven into the sea. The Welsh would be led by Cynan and Cadwaladr; while Cynan's credentials are not known, Cadwaladr was the son of Cadwallon who conquered Northumbria in the seventh century. Thomas Parry has written that, besides the element of prophecy, the poem also contains 'an earnestness of purpose, a fiery enthusiasm and a national self-consciousness', qualities which were to suffuse all the subsequent poetry of prophecy written in the middle ages.

The Norman advance into Wales in the twelfth century gave a new impetus to the validity of the poetry of prophecy. It was Geoffrey of Monmouth's *History of the Kings of Britain*, appearing in 1136, which cast the basic content of Welsh prophetic poetry into new and dynamic forms.

Geoffrey's *British History* stressed such potent themes as the common Welsh descent from Brutus, great-grandson of the Trojan hero Aeneas, and the greatness of a memorable national hero, King Arthur. There was also a national prophet, Merlin, a national emblem in the Red Dragon and an apparently authoritative prediction in Merlin's prophecies that the Red Dragon was to be ultimately

99

victorious. The age-old theme of eventual victory over the Saxons now received its definitive form in the *British History*, and 'hence regardless of its truth or falsehood, it is of supreme importance as a living force moulding and directing the conceptions and aspirations of the medieval Welshman'.[2]

It was this literary background that prepared the way for the emergence of Henry Tudor as the last of a long line of prophetic heroes. The ending of the ancient dynasty of Gwynedd in 1282–3 gave a new urgency to Geoffrey of Monmouth's visions. But the transmission of these prophecies and their crystallization around a specific political personage was the prerogative of the bardic class with their kindred links encompassing the whole of Wales. It was the poets who would marry prophecy to the politics of the Wars of the Roses.

The Bardic Class

Although the events of 1282–3 brought profound political changes to Wales, the social role of the bards continued in the new political context. In early medieval Wales bardic poets had a prominent legally defined place in the society of the little kingdoms. Princes and nobles wrote poetry and the Welsh legal code of Hywel Dda (Howell the Good, d. 950) listed among the principal officers of the royal court the chief bard (*pencerdd*). He was close to the throne and probably served as the King's official story-teller and historian.

Beneath the *pencerdd* was the household bard (*bardd teilu*) who sometimes served in the royal bodyguard. There was also a lesser constellation of minor poets and minstrels as part of the bardic organization. Patronized by the princes as an organic part of their administrative class, the bards were integral to society and acted as collective historians, propagandists and, not least, genealogists.

The collapse of the independent Welsh political structure during 1282–3 in both north and south Wales meant the ending of the official bardic organization. But the principle of patronage continued and the bards retained an important role in society. The poetry of the princes became the poetry of the *uchelwyr*, or gentry, who maintained the old traditions and kept alive the ancient Welsh literary culture. The bards survived by attaching themselves, often as itinerants, to the prominent gentry houses which straddled Wales from Anglesey to Gwent. As they moved from household to household, celebrating the virtues of their patron, the beauty of his wife and the distinction of his genealogy, the bards developed a national constituency.[3]

With the change in the social structure of bardic patronage, which reflected the growing importance of that gentry class which was to rally to the support of the Tudors, came a change in the more popular forms of poetry. The more formal metres of earlier Welsh poetry were loosened, and although much poetry continued to be written in the form of the *awdl* (ode), the *cywydd*, a flexible alliterative couplet, became increasingly popular in the fourteenth century. The *cywydd* could project the epigram, it was easier to memorize for recitation, and thus these qualities made it ideal for political propaganda.

During the relatively stable years of the early and mid-fourteenth century there was little overt anti-English feeling expressed by the classical or court poets of the *uchelwyr*. Their themes were love and nature, and Dafydd ap Gwilym, who epitomizes this class, came of a family that had long served the English crown. Indeed Dafydd ap Gwilym's own uncle was constable of Newcastle Emlyn in 1343.

But not all Welsh poetry of the fourteenth century was apolitical verse inspired by love or the beauties of the Welsh countryside. The poetry of prophecy had by no means died and it continued to be written in parallel with the court poetry of the gentry. As the political and racial tensions in Wales grew during the fourteenth century, the poetry of prophecy assumed ever-greater importance. Although much of this poetry was written anonymously or by bards who practised a deliberate obscurity for security reasons, the basic themes of a national messiah who would bring deliverance retained their potency.

Much of this poetry was written in allegory and in particular political leaders were often represented by the names of animals as in the 'Prophecies of Merlin' in Geoffrey's *British History*. Leopards, boars, dragons, bulls, eagles, ravens and serpents proliferated and the convention became increasingly popular. In the fifteenth century the poet Lewis Glyn Cothi collected between twenty and thirty allegorical animals in one ode. During the later stages of the Wars of the Roses, Richard III was invariably referred to by the Welsh poets as the Boar, from his favourite cognizance, while the Black Bull referred solely to either Jasper or Henry Tudor. Similarly, Rhys ap Thomas was invariably known as the Raven from the three heraldic ravens of the House of Dinefwr.

As the technical resources of the poetry of prophecy became more elaborate in this way, so the prophetic variant of the popular *cywydd* received its own distinctive designation, the *cywydd brud* or *brut*. This designation derived from 'a transferred use of Brut = Brutus' (*OED*), and meant originally a chronicle or history of the descendants of Brutus or simply a chronicle, as in *Brut Y Tywysogion* ('The Chronicle of the Princes').

During the fourteenth century the word in Welsh recovered its associations with the story of Brutus, the legendary founder of the British race, and 'is thus attached to the vaticinatory poetry which foretells the triumph of his descendants'.[4]

By the time of Owain Glyn Dŵr's rebellion a whole corpus of Welsh prophetic poetry thus existed with its own conventions, traditions, forms and even nomenclature, the *cywydd brud*. After the collapse of the great rebellion this poetry continued to develop, and eventually its entire resources were used to support Henry Tudor's bid for the throne.

The Search for a Saviour

During the late fourteenth century a significant development took place in the conventions of the poetry of prophecy. Instead of projecting a mythical or legendary hero of the past as the Son of Prophecy, poetry began to be written for the direct political purpose of canvassing the claims of a particular Welsh leader. One such leader was Owain Lawgoch (Red Hand), a direct descendant of the House of Gwynedd. His career read like a medieval romance, for while still a young man he had entered the service of Philip IV of France. Subsequently, he had made a great reputation for himself as a soldier of fortune in Brittany and Lombardy, as well as Alsace and Switzerland. On the Continent, he was known as 'Yevain de Galles' or Owain of Wales.

Although a comparative stranger to Wales, his hereditary claim was supported (and exploited) by the French court and plans were laid in the early 1370s for a landing in Wales under Owain's leadership. But the expedition got no further than Guernsey. Nevertheless, Owain was henceforth considered a menace by the English crown, and his death in France in 1378, at the hand of an assassin, was probably due to English connivance. The invasion threat thus passed, but Owain's fame lived on and he became a hero in both the French chronicles and the prophetic poetry of Wales.[5]

A generation after the death of the Red Hand, Owain Glyn Dŵr made his last, lost bid for Welsh independence. Glyn Dŵr's career touched on many aspects of prophecy and divination, as we have noted, and there can be little doubt that the Welsh leader saw himself as the national deliverer as foretold by the whole corpus of prophetic poetry.

After the collapse of the rebellion, any further hopes for the recovery of Welsh independence must have seemed unreal. But Glyn Dŵr's achievement of Welsh unity, a unity far more effective than any won by the Princes of Gwynedd, remained as an inspiration for the poets. According to one authority on the poetry of the period,

> this awakening of national consciousness produced a remarkable corpus of poetry. The poets in their eulogies of prospective leaders always saw in their inward eye the shape of Owain Glyn Dŵr. His star shines brightly in many a *cywydd*, the dash of a gallant squire was simply his pomp revived, his blood was the country's surest protection, the outlaws in the hills were his men, the braves of many battles were his wolves and lions . . .[6]

With the advent of the Wars of the Roses in mid-century, this new confidence of the bards (and their gentry patrons) received further encouragement. Wales became one of the most important cockpits of the dynastic struggle and both York and Lancaster tried to mobilize support there for their objectives. The poets were quickly aware of this change in the political scene and a new cycle of prophetic poetry was at hand. The bards now sought not so much a leader who would take Wales to independence, as a hero who would work within the English political system for the Welsh cause. Jasper Tudor and William Herbert were cast in this role before the emergence of Henry Tudor.[7]

Within this framework a large number of *cywyddau brud*, or prophetic poems, were written during the Wars of the Roses by such court or classical poets as Tudur Penllyn, Lewis Glyn Cothi, Guto'r

Glyn and in particular Dafydd Llwyd of Mathfarn. The classical poets came to embrace the poetry of prophecy, unlike their rather apolitical predecessors of the fourteenth century. Consequently most of the bardic class was now to become involved with the prophetic poetry and its heroes.

By the rules of his craft, a Welsh bard was bound to support his patron's loyalty to his overlord. But there was a distinct territorial aspect to this system of patronage. In general west Wales and the north were Lancastrian in sympathy, and thus the local bards would sing to Jasper Tudor or Gruffydd ap Nicholas who wrote poetry himself and who presided over the famous eisteddfod held in Carmarthen in about 1453. In the Mortimer lordships of the March the Yorkists were in the ascendant and the bards would naturally see in William Herbert a Son of Prophecy.

According to the fortunes of war, the same bard might successively praise the indestructible Jasper Tudor, William Herbert or Edward IV as the best champion of the Welsh cause. Lewis Glyn Cothi, for example, sang to Jasper, then to Edward IV before finally returning to the Tudors. The test was not a dynastic one as the bards sought a hero who would best advance Welsh interests. Eventually the poets, whether in west Wales or the Marches, whether Yorkist or Lancastrian, saw Henry Tudor as the champion best fitted to fill the role of Son of Prophecy.

During the early 1450s Gruffydd ap Nicholas emerged as an autonomous political force in his own right who could defy the crown with impunity. This development inspired Lewis Glyn Cothi (d. *c.* 1490) to view Gruffydd's rise as the beginning of a new era when 'the Saxon will no longer be found presiding over the Sessions or holding an official position amongst us'. As Jasper Tudor came into the leadership of the Lancastrian cause in Pembroke and west Wales during the later 1450s, he was praised by Lewis Glyn Cothi for his Welsh extraction, for his royal blood and his care for his young ward Henry Tudor, and for his efforts to unite Wales for Henry VI.

One of the most prominent bards of the period, Lewis took his name from the great forest of Glyn Cothi in north Carmarthenshire, where he was probably brought up at Pwllcynbyd in the parish of Llanybyther. Nearby were Newton and Dinefwr, the home and estate of Gruffydd ap Nicholas, who was one of Lewis Glyn Cothi's leading patrons. In his turn, the poet sang Gruffydd's praises with true bardic fervour . . . 'Great as is his revenue in Wales, still greater are his possessions . . . he overflowed Dinefwr . . . ere he grew to man's estate.'

On the whole Lewis Glyn Cothi sided with the Lancastrians and he was probably outlawed, on account of his loyalty to Jasper Tudor, after the Battle of Mortimer's Cross in 1461. Much of Lewis Glyn Cothi's best work is dedicated to patrons in Carmarthenshire and Cardiganshire, although his works indicate that most parts of Wales and the Borders were known to him.

Lewis Glyn Cothi's loyalty to Jasper Tudor did not prevent him from putting his muse at the disposal of Yorkist patrons during the ascendancy of the White Rose after 1461. He praised Edward IV as 'a royal Welshman' and asked him to rid Wales of oppression. Edward was descended from Gwladys Ddu, the Dark (d. 1251), daughter of Llewellyn the Great who had married Ralph Mortimer of Wigmore (d. 1246). The Yorkist king was therefore entitled to Welsh support as being in the true Brutus line. Lewis Glyn Cothi was thus quite consistent in his nationalism and towards the end of his life returned to his first loyalty, the Tudors. He then fervently supported the cause of Henry and Jasper Tudor immediately preceding Bosworth.[8]

Another famous bard of the period whose work linked prophecy and politics was Guto'r Glyn (d. c. 1493). He was brought up in Glyn Ceiriog near Llangollen and was drawn to Oswestry as his metropolis, although he also wrote of Anglesey, Gwynedd and Gwent. Politically a man of the Marches, and also Powys, where Mortimer influence was strong, Guto'r Glyn was a steady supporter of the Yorkist cause. His chief hero was William Herbert of Raglan, Earl of Pembroke, executed after the disaster of Banbury in 1469. But Guto'r Glyn was also fond of churchmen such as the Abbot of Shrewsbury and he died at Valle Crucis Abbey near Llangollen.

Like Lewis Glyn Cothi, Guto'r Glyn sang to Edward IV as a descendant of Gwladys Ddu, and called on the Yorkist king to 'Restore order, come thyself, valiant Edward, and check the oppressors . . .' The fact of Edward's Welsh blood, however diluted, was of great importance to Guto'r Glyn, but although he was attracted to the King and wore his badge, his primary loyalty was reserved for William Herbert. Clearly, for Guto'r Glyn, the Welsh Yorkist leader was a Son of Prophecy.

As we have seen, Guto'r Glyn called on Herbert after the fall of Harlech Castle in 1468 to make 'Glamorgan and Gwynedd, from Conway to Neath, an United Whole'. The poet also asked Herbert not to avenge himself on the Lancastrian garrison of Harlech (whom he considered Welsh patriots) but to use his prestige to free Wales from the Saxon yoke.

Herbert was created Earl of Pembroke after the fall of Harlech. But Guto'r Glyn was full of foreboding when Herbert was summoned to Edward's side after Warwick's revolt in 1469. He warned his great patron that 'the children of Rowena' had hatred for him; following Herbert's execution after Banbury, Guto'r Glyn wrote that 'my nation is destroyed, now that the Earl is slain'. With Warwick's own death at the Battle of Barnet in 1471, Guto'r Glyn, as a representative writer, regarded it as an occasion for national rejoicing and as just retribution for Herbert's execution.[9] But with Herbert's end and Jasper Tudor's exile, there was no champion of Welsh interests available to fill the poetic role of Son of Prophecy.

The final stages of the Wars of the Roses, however, saw a great rallying of the poets around the person of Henry Tudor. This support came from Yorkist and Lancastrian bards alike, from the supporters of Jasper Tudor and William Herbert. There were sound historical reasons for this phenomenon.

It will be recalled that the main Lancastrian line had been eliminated with the death of Henry VI and his heir, Prince Edward, in 1471. Henry Tudor was now the residual Lancastrian claimant through his mother, Margaret Beaufort. But the Yorkists could still draw considerable support in Wales. Edward IV, after all, was regarded even by the Lancastrian Lewis Glyn Cothi as worthy of Welsh support on account of his descent from Gwladys Ddu and the Mortimers. He was 'a royal Welshman' of the Brutus line.

But this reasoning was no longer valid with the usurpation of Richard III and the death of the Princes in the Tower. Edward IV's heirs were in the Brutus line too and with their death the Welsh Yorkists had no true dynastic leader. A transfer of loyalty to Richard III was impossible as the full implications of the usurpation became apparent.

Thus by 1485 there was little real support in Wales for Richard III, not even from those traditional Yorkists, the Herberts and the Vaughans of south-east Wales and the Marches. The bards and their patrons were in full agreement, and all the resources of poetry and politics converged on Henry Tudor who now became the ultimate Son of Prophecy. The most famous poet of the time, Dafydd Llwyd ap Llewellyn of Mathafarn (d. *c.* 1500), who was also the most ardent and influential bardic supporter of Henry, castigated Richard III 'as a servile boar who, in his wardship did imprison the Sons of Edward and kill his two nephews who were young. Shame on the hang-lipped Saracen for slaying the angels of Christ . . .'[10]

Prince and Poet

In Dafydd Llwyd the tradition of prophecy reached its historic culmination. He was the accomplished author of some fifty of the 200 prophetic poems which survive from his generation, and was famed as a seer and interpreter of the Welsh prophetic books. He was also a soldier and a huntsman and was born, like his wife Margaret, of leading gentry stock.

Dafydd Llwyd praised both Dafydd ap Ieuan ap Einon, the Lancastrian defender of Harlech Castle, and William Herbert who had taken the castle in 1468. He was less concerned with dynastic politics than with the opportunities offered to the Welsh cause by the upheaval of the Wars of the Roses. But as the civil war reached its climax after the usurpation of Richard III, Dafydd Llwyd became a staunch supporter of the Lancastrian cause and saw Henry Tudor as his greatest hero.[11]

The poet's praises for Henry were written for his patron-chieftains and were designed to enlist the maximum support from the natural leaders of society who would see in the Tudor one of their own. The appeal was to national sentiment and to a high leader of ancient lineage, rather than to any conceptual nationalism. Dafydd Llwyd praised Henry and Jasper Tudor as true Sons of Prophecy and leaders 'of the stock of Cadwaladr, the bright ray'. Thus the Brutus line would be truly fulfilled by Henry's victory.

The convergence of politics and prophecy was apparently complete when, according to tradition, the new Cadwaladr stayed overnight at Mathafarn during his march from Dale to Bosworth to consult with the poet and prophet. Following Bosworth Field, Henry VII made Dafydd Llwyd an Esquire of the Body, while the poet certainly believed that the ancient prophecies of the Welsh destiny had been fulfilled by his hero's victory. He sang of Henry that 'No one reached as high as he; under heaven no man will go higher.'[12]

Of the period preceding Henry Tudor's landing in August 1485, one historian, A. H. Dodd, has noted that 'there was no limit to the prospects opened for Wales in the eyes of his enthusiastic supporters who dreamt of the Britain of Geoffrey of Monmouth come to life again . . .' Another authority, E. D. Jones, considers that

> in the burst of prophetic frenzy after 1483, Dafydd Llwyd was as eloquent as any of the disciples of Geoffrey of Monmouth in conjuring the illusion that Welsh nationalism would be crowned in London. Vaticination had been an element in the works of the classic poets, now it ran wild . . .[13]

Yet a central paradox in the complex relationship between prophecy and politics was that the messianic anticipations of the poets were not shared by their ambitious, realistic sponsors. Such leading politicians as Rhys ap Thomas hoped to achieve limited, material objectives rather than fulfil the prophecies of Geoffrey of Monmouth. The patrons of prophecy were considerably more hard-headed than its practitioners. Above all, although Henry Tudor took the supreme gamble in 1485, and although he retained a fascination with things Welsh, he was a shrewd, calculating ruler, 'a wonder for wise men' in Francis Bacon's famous words. The visions of the prophetic poetry had thus little place in Henry's practical concern with keeping the throne he was to win at Bosworth.

The Welsh gentry who sponsored and encouraged the bards thus had mixed motives. They believed in national sentiment, certainly, but they also hoped for royal favour, the ending of legal discrimination and other advantages accruing once the victorious Son of Prophecy was on the throne of England. They saw in their champion, Henry Tudor – as earlier some of them had seen in Jasper Tudor or William Herbert – a leader who could reconcile their interests with that of the crown.

Hence the psychological union between England and Wales which occurred at Bosworth was finally consummated in the legislative union wrought by Henry Tudor's son. Then the Welsh gentry's position as the natural leaders of society was finally underwritten by Parliament. Bosworth was a victory which led to reconciliation rather than to the revenge which was implicit in the prophetic poetry.[14]

The corollary was that after Bosworth the influence of the bards declined. Dafydd Llwyd, with his visionary projection of Henry Tudor, was the last great practitioner of prophecy. Henry VII's successors were only too aware of the lethal implications of the political prophecy which had helped put the Tudor dynasty on the throne. When Rhys ap Thomas's grandson, the ill-starred Rhys ap Gruffydd, was thought to have prophesied that the Red Hand of Scotland and the Ravens of Dinefwr would conquer England he aroused the suspicions of Henry VIII and lost his head in 1531.

But during the summer of 1485, prophecy and politics merged as never before. The bards were aware of Henry of Richmond's preparations at the mouth of the Seine. In an 'Ode to St David', Dafydd Llwyd was fired by the vision of victory . . . 'And the city of England will be reduced under thee; the world will be driven, the Boar made cold . . .'

The veteran poet Lewis Glyn Cothi was even more impatient for the coming of Henry's expedition from France, as he sang to Jasper Tudor:

> In what seas are thy anchors, and where art
>   thou thyself?
> When wilt thou, Black Bull, come to land;
> How long shall we wait?
> On the Feast of the Virgin, fair Gwynedd in her
>   singing,
> Watched the seas. . . .[15]

8

Henry's Welsh Ally

Rhys ap Thomas, the chief Welsh supporter of Henry Tudor, was the grandson of Gruffydd ap Nicholas who had exercised virtually independent power in west Wales during the 1440s and 1450s. The founder of the House of Dinefwr had been overshadowed by the rising star of Jasper Tudor later in the 1450s and Gruffydd ap Nicholas had died in about 1460.

Gruffydd had been married three times to the daughters of Welsh gentry families. His first marriage was to Mabel, daughter of Maredudd ap Henry Dwnn of Kidwelly, his second marriage was to Margaret, third daughter of Sir Thomas Perrot, and his third marriage was to Jane, daughter of Jenkin ap Rhys of Gilfach Wen near Llandysul. Jenkin had been a crown officer in Cardiganshire during the early years of Henry VI.

From these three marriages Gruffydd had three surviving sons. Of John little is known save that he joined his father in leasing the Dinefwr lands between 1439 and 1456.

Owain was more in the activist mould of his father serving as his lieutenant in the Pembroke region during the 1450s. He was also one of the leaders of the Lancastrian force during the last siege of Carreg Cennen Castle during 1461–2. Owain ap Gruffydd ap Nicholas was the heir to Cwrt Bryn-y-Beirdd ('The Hill of the Bards'), a house which stands in a commanding position about one mile south of Carreg Cennen Castle.

It was through Gruffydd ap Nicholas's third son, Thomas, that his line passed to Rhys ap Thomas.[1]

During the zenith of Gruffydd ap Nicholas's influence in west Wales, Thomas had represented his father in Cardiganshire where he became the deputy sheriff of that royal county as well as deputy constable of Aberystwyth Castle. With the death of his father, Thomas had attempted to assert his own influence in Carmarthenshire. He was farmer of Dinefwr during 1460–1, and he also probably inherited Gruffydd ap Nicholas's residence at Newton. With his brother Owain, Thomas headed the Lancastrian garrison at Carreg Cennen during 1461–2.

After the surrender of this last Lancastrian stronghold in west Wales during the summer of 1462, the local influence of the sons of Gruffydd ap Nicholas was superseded by the power of the Yorkists. The House of Dinefwr was overshadowed by the Yorkist leader in Wales, William Herbert. Thomas ap Gruffydd was relegated to a secondary position. But he retained many of the estates of Gruffydd ap Nicholas, even regaining possession of the Dinefwr lands after the surrender of Carreg Cennen.

The Blood of the Raven

Despite the loss of political influence under Yorkist rule, Thomas ap Gruffydd made a significant marriage which was to have considerable influence on the fortunes of his son Rhys. He took to wife, at some time before 1446, Elizabeth, daughter of Sir John Gruffydd of Abermarlais in the parish of Llansadwrn, about six miles north-east of Llandeilo, and near the route from Hereford and Brecon to Carmarthen.

Sir John Gruffydd was a direct descendant of Gruffydd, son of Ednyfed Fychan, seneschal of Gwynedd and Gwenllian, daughter of the Lord Rhys. Sir John possessed extensive estates in England, but the west Wales parts of his inheritance passed to Elizabeth on her marriage to Thomas ap Gruffydd. Elizabeth's lands included not only the Abermarlais estate but other holdings at Llanrhystyd in Cardiganshire. These lands, like Abermarlais, descended ultimately to the Gruffydd family from Ednyfed Fychan the Seneschal. Other lands inherited by Elizabeth Gruffydd included properties at Betws Bledrws and Llangybi near Lampeter in Cardiganshire.

Abermarlais was an historic house well known to the bards. The poet Lewis Glyn Cothi described a tournament held at Abermarlais attended by Thomas ap Gruffydd's son and his retainers. Other gentry families, the Mansels, the Bassets and the Ryds, were present, armed with bows, crossbows, battle-axes and maces . . . 'Colourful heraldic pencels and standards waved over the lists, foremost among them the raven banner of Abermarlais . . .'[2]

Thomas ap Gruffydd did not long survive his father. He was killed in an armed encounter at Pennal, near Machynlleth, perhaps during William Herbert's campaign against Harlech Castle in 1468. After the death of Thomas, who was predeceased by his two elder sons, Rhys ap Thomas succeeded to the combined estates of Newton, with the Dinefwr lands, and Abermarlais.

In addition to inheriting these and other properties, Rhys ap Thomas was the political beneficiary of his mother's descent from Ednyfed Fychan and Gwenllian. His lineage had the historic associations of the Lord Rhys and the princes of Deheubarth that so appealed to the bards. Moreover, there was kinship with the royal Tudors. In an ode to Rhys ap Thomas, the poet Lewis Glyn Cothi, that indefatigable laureate of the House of Dinefwr, sang that while Henry VII was descended from Goronwy, Rhys was descended from Gruffydd, both sons of Ednyfed Fychan.[3]

Rhys ap Thomas was born in 1449 and died in 1525, the virtual Tudor viceroy of south Wales. As a young man he had spent some time with his father, Thomas, in the Burgundian court. Here Rhys followed the profession of arms before returning to Wales in about 1467. His upbringing in general followed a pattern common to many late medieval gentlemen.

His first wife was Eva, daughter of Henry ap Gwilym of Court Henry, a fifteenth-century house about five miles west of Dinefwr. Rhys's second wife was Janet, daughter of Thomas Mathew of Raydr in Glamorgan, who was the widow of another Glamorgan landowner, Thomas Stradling of St Donats.[4]

Although Rhys ap Thomas maintained Newton as a residence, most of his youth was probably spent at Abermarlais, his mother's home. Surrounded by rolling parkland, the house looked eastwards over the Tywi valley to the hills of Cantref Bychan and the Black Mountain.

The poets Guto'r Glyn and Tudur Aled addressed their *cywyddau* to Rhys ap Thomas at Abermarlais. The house was later described by the Tudor antiquary, John Leland, as 'a well favoured stone place, moated, now mended, and augmented by Sir Rhys ap Thomas'. After 1485, when he acquired great political power in Wales, Rhys made Carew Castle, near Pembroke, his chief residence. He also acquired Carreg

Cennen Castle, Newcastle Emlyn and Weobley Castle in Gower, where he owned the manor of Landimore.

But poets and genealogists continued to refer to his family as 'The Blood of the Raven' (*Gwaed Y Fran*). This was a reference to the famous armorial bearings of the House of Dinefwr, *argent, between a chevron, three ravens sable.*

Rhys ap Thomas's family tradition in the Wars of the Roses was Lancastrian. But clearly, accommodation to Yorkist rule was politic during the reign of Edward IV; Rhys is said to have organized a local military force on behalf of the Yorkist king.

If Rhys was in the political wilderness during the Yorkist period, there can be little doubt that he worked with an almost ruthless dedication to maintain and expand his estates. One chronicler, Ellis Griffith, later wrote that Rhys and his family had

> many a deep curse from the poor people who were neighbours, for depriving them of their houses, lands and riches. For I heard the conversation of folk from that part of the country who said that no common people owned land within twenty miles from the dwelling of old Sir Rhys son of Thomas. If he desired such lands he would appropriate them without payment or thanks, and the disinherited doubtless cursed him . . .[5]

Rhys ap Thomas's landed interests were not confined to Carmarthenshire, for he also held land in Pembrokeshire and Cardiganshire. In the latter county, he held property in Cardigan town and Aberystwyth, besides the Cardiganshire estates inherited from his mother. Even before Bosworth, Rhys had therefore recaptured much of the regional prestige and power of his grandfather, Gruffydd ap Nicholas.

When the time came in the summer of 1485, it was these extensive west Wales estates of Rhys ap Thomas that enabled him to raise 'the great bande of soldiers' referred to in Polydore Vergil's account of the march to Bosworth.

Rhys Supports Henry Tudor

Probably some time soon after the usurpation of Richard III in June 1483, Rhys ap Thomas made the decision to join the conspiracy which led to Buckingham's revolt later that year. An interesting, but not completely reliable, source of these events is the Rice family history written by one of Rhys ap Thomas's descendants, Henry Rice of Newton (d. *c.* 1651) and entitled 'The Life of Rhys ap Thomas'.[6] (The family name was anglicized to Rice at the end of the sixteenth century, but changed back to Rhys in 1911.)

The 'Life' is partly an attempt to clear the name of Sir Rhys ap Gruffydd, Rhys ap Thomas's grandson executed for treason in 1531. Many of the details, drawn from family traditions regarding both Gruffydd ap Nicholas and Rhys ap Thomas, are probably accurate. But there is no evidence that Rhys ap Thomas met Henry Tudor at the landing at Dale in August 1485, as is asserted in the 'Life'.

According to the 'Life', Rhys ap Thomas's tutor during his youth was Edward Lewis, the Welsh-born physician, educated at Padua, who later ministered to Lady Margaret Beaufort. He was thus able to travel to Abermarlais without suspicion and was instrumental in drawing Rhys ap Thomas into the conspiracy. Lewis also helped in reconciling Rhys with the Duke of Buckingham, for the two men had 'a deadlie quarrel'.

The reconciliation between the two magnates, as almost between two warring powers, took place on the route from Brecon to Abermarlais at Trecastle, near the western borders of Buckingham's lordship of Brecon. Rhys ap Thomas looked forward to 'an alteration in the state', but apparently he took no overt part in Buckingham's abortive rebellion. The main focus of the revolt was in any case in the south of England, well away from Rhys's domain.

Subsequently Rhys ap Thomas, who held no office under Richard III, and who was able to mobilize support for Henry Tudor solely on account of his personal ascendancy, aroused the suspicion of the King. Richard III asked Rhys for the custody of his son as a hostage. But the Welshman was able to circumvent this demand by assuring Richard that Henry Tudor 'must resolve with himself to make his entrance and irruption over my bellie'. Hence the later but apocryphal story that Rhys ap Thomas stood under Mullock Bridge, on the way from Dale to Haverfordwest, while Richmond and his forces passed overhead.

As the renewed conspiracy against Richard gathered increasing support during 1484–5, Rhys ap Thomas was approached by John Morgan (later Bishop of St David's) and his brother Morgan of

Kidwelly. A relative of the Morgan brothers, Evan Morgan, had already fled to Brittany after the collapse of Buckingham's revolt to join his friend Jasper Tudor.

Another local member of the conspiracy was Arnold Butler of Coedcanlas near Pembroke. Also involved was the Abbot of Talley, who may have been counsellor to Rhys ap Thomas. He eased Rhys ap Thomas's conscience over his impending rebellion. The grand objective of these activities was of course to see that Rhys delivered to Richmond 'the keys of that part of the kingdom'.

Eventually, as we have noted, John Morgan sent word to Henry Tudor in France that Rhys ap Thomas and the Cheshire landowner John Savage 'were wholly given to Earl Henry's affairs' (Polydore Vergil).

Presumably it was in the weeks immediately preceding Richmond's landing at Dale that Rhys ap Thomas decided on his line of advance to Shrewsbury. The route was to lie through Carmarthen, Llandovery and Brecon, towns mentioned in this context in the 'Life'. From Brecon, Rhys probably planned to march north across the Eppynt Hills to Builth and so along the upper Wye and upper Severn valleys to Welshpool and Shrewsbury.

It was a cleverly planned route as it enabled Rhys ap Thomas to cover Richmond's main line of advance along the Cardiganshire coast. At the same time this route enabled Rhys to recruit support from dissentient Yorkists in the March.

Many of the details of the Welsh side of the conspiracy will never be known. But considerable preparations must have been made for Rhys to mobilize his forces immediately on Richmond's landing, then proceed on a difficult route northwards towards Shrewsbury.

A number of influential Welshmen must have been involved in the venture. For obvious reasons, great secrecy would have been necessary, a secrecy which has continued to hide Rhys ap Thomas's full involvement. But what is certain is that Rhys ap Thomas played a brave and important part in the campaign that culminated at Bosworth Field on 22 August 1485.

Of Rhys's motives in commiting himself to Henry Tudor, we can only speculate. National sentiment, certainly, must have played a part, as well as perhaps the kinship tie between the Tudors and Rhys ap Thomas. But Rhys was also the grandson of Gruffydd ap Nicholas, his family had been in the political wilderness during the Yorkist era, and ambition, calculation, and self-interest must have played a part in his decision. No doubt Rhys believed that his own interests were inseparable from those of his class in supporting Henry Tudor.

For Rhys ap Thomas the rewards accruing from his decision to support Henry Tudor, once the God of Battles had settled the issue at Bosworth, were considerable. Knighted after Bosworth, he was made chamberlain of south Wales three months later. This was the first of a series of awards that led to his creation as a Knight of the Garter in 1505.

But Rhys's rewards were not only material ones. His support for Henry Tudor was welcomed by Yorkist and Lancastrian bards alike. Guto'r Glyn sang of his prowess at Bosworth and how the ravens had prepared the victory. Lewis Glyn Cothi even attributed to Rhys ap Thomas personally the slaying of Richard III.[7]

Welsh poets, of course, praised Rhys as a champion of Welsh interests at Bosworth. But there are also many favourable references to Rhys by English chroniclers of the Tudor period who lauded his role in the making of the new monarchy.

Eventually, in the famous closing scenes of *Richard III*, Shakespeare noted Rhys's part in the triumph of the red rose:

STANLEY: . . . But tell me, where is princely Richmond now?
URSWICK: At Pembroke or at Ha'rfordwest in Wales.
STANLEY: What men of note resort to him?
URSWICK: Sir Walter Herbert, a renowned soldier,
  Sir Gilbert Talbot, Sir William Stanley
  Oxford, redoubted Pembroke, Sir James Blunt,
  And Rice ap Thomas with a valiant crew;
  And many other of great name and worth;
  And towards London do they bend their power . . .

To be sure, a fleeting reference. Yet in this way, the greatest of Englishmen immortalized the role of Henry Tudor's Welsh ally on the road to Bosworth.

9

The Road to Bosworth

On 1 August 1485 Henry Tudor sailed from Harfleur for Wales with his expeditionary force. Henry was probably accompanied by a few hundred devoted English exiles who had made their way to join him in Brittany and France.

The bulk of the force was composed of some 2,000 Frenchmen, perhaps more, who were described by the contemporary chronicler Philip de Commines as the worst rabble that could be found. However, Charles Ross has shown in his recent biography of Richard III that Commines' dismissal of these men was hardly justified. Most of the French troops who sailed with Henry Tudor were seasoned professionals, paid by the French government, and discharged from the 'huge and expensive' military base at Pont de l'Arche in the Seine valley. There was also a contingent of Scots and some Breton adventurers.

Moreover, the French commander, Philibert de Chandée, was an experienced veteran known to Henry from the early days of his exile. He was knighted by Henry, along with some of Richmond's closest English supporters, on landing in Wales, and the French commander was further awarded with the earldom of Bath in 1486. These honours suggest that Henry Tudor was not displeased with the performance of his French troops on the Bosworth campaign.

The Landing at Mill Bay

Helped by a soft southerly wind, Henry's fleet made a landfall at St Ann's Head soon before sundown on 7 August 1485. His force then disembarked at Mill Bay, the first cove on the north side of Milford Haven. The bay lies about a quarter of a mile south of Brunt farm, and nearly two miles south of Dale Castle and village.

The Road to Bosworth

A small force of Henry Tudor's men may have landed at the opposite side of Milford Haven at the cove now known as West Angle Bay. From here these men could have advanced against Pembroke and Tenby Castles (see map, p. 120).

Many historians have described Henry's landing as taking place at Dale or in Milford Haven itself. But local tradition, combined with the special military advantages of Mill Bay, pinpoints Henry Tudor's landing place as this small sandstone cove. Polydore Vergil significantly writes that Henry did not land at Dale but that, entering Milford Haven on the evening of 7 August, he 'forthwith' landed and first took a place called Dale that same evening. Caution was indicated, Polydore Vergil notes, because at Dale 'certain companies of his adversaries had had their station the winter by past to have kept him from landing'.

Pembrokeshire historians and local tradition have long focussed on Mill Bay as the historic site of the landing in 1485. George Owen of Henllys, whose well-known work, *The Description of Pembrokeshire*, was completed before 1602, noted that 'neare this point of Dale, between yt and the towne of Dale, landed King Henry 7th and his Armye from Brytanne when he came into England and conquered King Richard the third . . .'

The Victorian historian of Pembrokeshire, Edward Laws, wrote that

> According to local tradition, Henry landed at Brunt, close to St Ann's head; indeed he is reported to have named the place, saying as he climbed over the rocks, 'This is Brunt', i.e., hard or difficult. At the present day the word 'brunt' is not to be found in our Pembrokeshire vocabulary, nor can I find that it ever was employed here or elsewhere as an adjective. Probably the place-name Brunt existed long before Tudor times. Perhaps Henry was familiar with the name and made a pun on the brunt of battle, as he was scrambling up the cliff.

Another Victorian writer on Pembrokeshire, Thornhill Timmins, repeats the story of Henry's exclamation at Brunt, and specifically names Mill Bay as 'the traditional landing place of Henry of Richmond'.[1]

What were the precise advantages of Mill Bay? In a detailed examination of the site, S. B. Chrimes has noted that Mill Bay is 'entirely invisible from Dale Point, Roads, Beach and Castle'. The Bay is separated from Dale by two promontories (West Blockhouse Point and Watwick Point) and by two coves (Watwick Bay and Castlebeach Bay). The ascent from these two coves is very much steeper than the climb from Mill Bay to Brunt and the road to Dale.[2]

Professor Chrimes wrote that the point on the beach at Mill Bay nearest Brunt was still known (1964) as Henry's Carthouse, and 'this according to local tradition is the precise spot where Henry landed'. The site today is partly covered by a rock fall, but on the other side of the beach are the remains of an old mill which may have given the bay its name. According to George Owen, the bay was known as Mill Bay at least as early as 1595.

Henry Tudor had spent much of his youth at Pembroke Castle, and it appears quite likely that the geography of Milford Haven would have been known to him. Furthermore, Mill Bay was in the barony of Walwyn's Castle, a member of Jasper Tudor's lordship of Pembroke on the north side of Milford Haven.

Accordingly, Chrimes considers that 'the best location for a secretive landing planned to enable an advance to Haverfordwest the next day was thus undoubtedly the beach now known as Mill Bay'. The whole of Dale Beach and Dale Roads is fully visible from Dale Castle and 'no leader of an expedition desirous of achieving secrecy and surprise would have dreamt of landing there'.

It was from Mill Bay, then, that Henry Tudor and his men scrambled up the track to Brunt at the beginning of their great adventure. From Brunt, Henry quickly advanced to Dale, less than two miles away, for the night of 7 August 1485.

If tactical reasons governed the choice for landing at Mill Bay, there were broader strategic reasons for landing north of Milford Haven and marching through Haverfordwest and along the Cardiganshire coast to Shrewsbury. Pembroke Castle, which guarded the route to Carmarthen from the south side of Milford Haven, had been made ready by Richard III. In January 1484 one of the ushers of Richard's chamber, Richard Williams, had been appointed constable and steward of the castles of Pembroke, Tenby, Haverfordwest, Manorbier and Cilgerran, on the Teifi near Cardigan. The office of constable of Pembroke Castle was to be held personally by Williams.

Pembroke Castle had been subsequently victualled and the

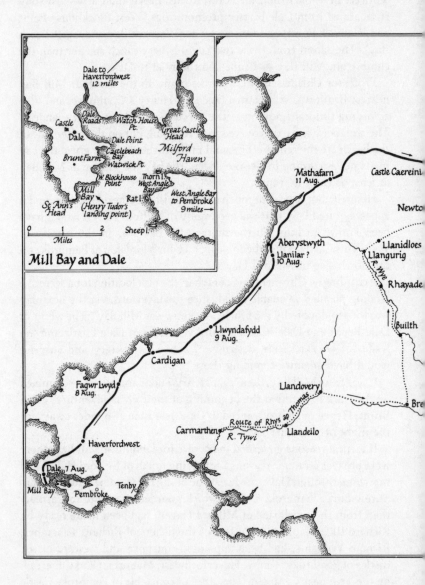

Dale to
Haverfordwest
12 miles

Dale
Roads

Castle
Dale

Watch House
Pt.

Dale Point

Brunt Farm

Castlebeach
Bay

Watwick Pt.

W. Blockhouse
Point

Mill
Bay

St. Ann's
Head

(Henry Tudor's
landing point)

Rat I.

Great Castle
Head

Milford
Haven

Thorn I.
West Angle
Bay

West Angle Bay
to Pembroke
9 miles

Sheep I.

0   1   2
Miles

Mill Bay and Dale

Mathafarn
11 Aug.

Castle Caereini

Newto

Aberystwyth

Llanilar ?
10 Aug.

Llanidloes
Llangurig

R. Wye

Rhayade

Builth

Llwyndafydd
9 Aug.

Cardigan

Fagwr Lwyd
8 Aug.

Llandovery

Bre

Route of Rhys ap Thomas

Carmarthen

R. Tywi

Llandeilo

Haverfordwest

Dale, 7 Aug.

Mill Bay

Pembroke

Tenby

120

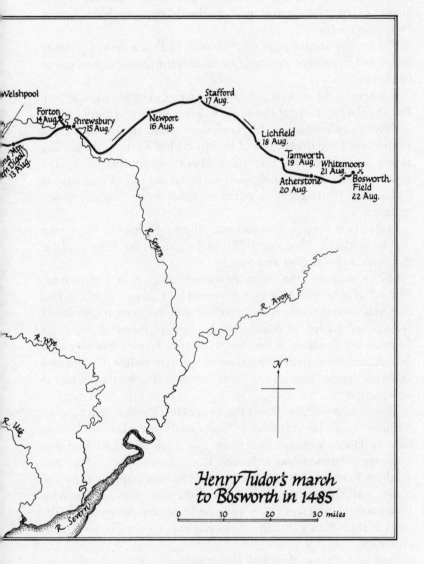

Welshpool

Forton
14 Aug.

Shrewsbury
15 Aug.

Newport
16 Aug.

Stafford
17 Aug.

Lichfield
18 Aug.

Tamworth
19 Aug.

Whitemoors
21 Aug.

Atherstone
20 Aug.

Bosworth
Field
22 Aug.

R. Severn

R. Avon

R. Wye

R. Usk

R. Severn

N

*Henry Tudor's march
to Bosworth in 1485*

0   10   20   30 *miles*

chamberlain of Carmarthen had been ordered to pay one Richard Newton £113 14s. 6d. for strengthening the castle. Firewood in large quantities from the forest near Narberth had also been sent to Pembroke Castle.

The landing at Mill Bay and the seizure of Dale meant that Henry Tudor and his forces were able to circumvent these preparations at Pembroke.

But despite the natural seclusion of Henry's landing place at Mill Bay and the avoidance of Pembroke by his main force, Henry had not achieved complete secrecy. It appears to be certain that either Richard Williams at Pembroke or one of his officers had learnt of the landing almost immediately and then taken steps to inform Richard III. The speed with which this intelligence was conveyed within four days to Richard at Nottingham, about 200 miles from Pembroke, was remarkable.

Evidently in the person of Richard Williams, Richard III had at least one loyal Welsh adherent; Williams fought on the King's side at Bosworth and was later attainted.[3]

On 11 August 1485, from Beskwood Lodge near Nottingham, Richard III wrote to Henry Vernon, one of his Esquires, to inform him that 'rebells and traitours accompanied with our ancient enemies of France' had landed 'at Nangle besides Milford Haven in Wales on Soneday last passed, as we be credibly informed, entending oure uttre destruction, the extreme subversion of this oyre realme . . .' Richard called on Vernon 'horssed and harneised' to rally to him 'in all hast to you possible . . .'[4]

This letter establishes firmly the date of Henry's landing as Sunday, 7 August 1485. The reference to Angle points to a subsidiary landing here by Henry's forces. This belief may have misled Richard into expecting a Tudor advance through Pembroke and Carmarthen into southern England. But Henry's advance had been carefully chosen to obtain both the maximum secrecy and the maximum support from Wales and the Marches before entering England at Shrewsbury. The route of this advance through Wales was to prove a major asset in his campaign.

Early on 8 August, therefore, Henry and his small army left Dale for Haverfordwest, twelve miles distant. The march to Bosworth had begun.

The March Through Wales

At daybreak on 8 August, Henry Tudor's forces left Dale for Haverfordwest. According to Polydore Vergil, here 'he was received with great goodwill by all men'. He was also joined by Arnold Butler of Coedcanlas (near Pembroke) who brought a few men and pledged the citizens of Pembroke 'who were ready to serve Jasper as their earl'. The success of Henry's venture now depended on whether he could march through Wales without meeting serious opposition from Richard III's forces.

From Haverfordwest, Henry departed north-eastwards for Cardigan, twenty-six miles distant, over the Preseli Hills. The Croyland chronicle noted that the King's opponents, 'having landed at Milford Haven in Wales, made their way through rugged and indirect tracts in the northern part of the province'. The route chosen by Henry and Jasper was now to bring them within six days of leaving Dale to the gates of Shrewsbury, about 150 miles away.

After leaving Haverfordwest, Henry quickly advanced five miles towards Cardigan. Then a rumour swept through his army that Walter Herbert and Rhys ap Thomas were at the head of a large force loyal to Richard III at Carmarthen. Henry's scouts, however, reported that all was quiet, and the danger passed. Henry was now soon joined by Richard Griffith, 'a man of high parentage', and by his pledged supporter, John Morgan. The march continued under the Red Dragon standard of Cadwaladr, later described by the Tudor chronicler Edward Hall as 'a red fiery dragon beaten upon green and white sarcenet'.

After crossing the ridge of the Preseli Hills at Bwlch-y-Gwynt, the Pass of the Wind, Henry entered the lordship of Cemaes. Tradition fixes Henry's resting place for 8 August as Fagwr Lwyd, south of Cilgwyn in the parish of Nevern. The site lies in a commanding position about a mile from the Cardigan road. Although abandoned as a farmstead in the early twentieth century, the ruins of Fagwr Lwyd remain marked by a clump of tall beech trees visible for many miles.[5]

Continuing the march north on 9 August, Henry crossed the Teifi at Cardigan in the shadow of the great royal castle. Here he is supposed to have rested briefly at the Three Mariners. At about this stage of the march, Henry sent a message to his mother, Lady Margaret Beaufort, and to the Stanleys telling them of his intention to cross the Severn and advance through Shropshire to London.

But Thomas, Lord Stanley, Lady Margaret's husband, steward of Richard III's household, had to move carefully. He had only been allowed to depart to his Lancashire home at Lathom by sending his son, George, Lord Strange, as a hostage to Richard III at Nottingham. Richard had taken up position at this central strategic point in June 1485, not being sure where Richmond would land. The King had sent for the Great Seal to facilitate the array of his forces at the end of July. It was not until 11 August that the King was told of Henry's landing.

From Cardigan, Henry continued what must have been a difficult march as he advanced along the coastal route in the direction of Aberystwyth and Machynlleth. There is a local tradition that his forces stopped for watering at Ffynnondewi at the fourteenth milestone north-east of Cardigan.

An even firmer tradition, accepted by many antiquarians, asserts that Henry Tudor stayed for the night of 9 August 1485 at the nearby house of Llwyndafydd in the parish of Llandysillio-gogo. His resting place was probably the house now called Neuadd (The Hall) which stands high over a narrow, secluded valley which runs down to Cardigan Bay at Cwmtydu, about two miles south of Newquay.

Henry's host at Llwyndafydd was Dafydd ap Ieuan, a descendant of Cadifor ap Dinawal, Lord of Castell Hywel in south Cardiganshire, himself a descendant of the famous chieftain Tudwal Gloff, son of Rhodri the Great. Dafydd ap Ieuan was thus a representative of that ancient class of Welsh gentry to which Henry had appealed. At Lwyndafydd, if the tradition is to believed, Henry was entertained in high style. After his accession, Henry sent his former host at Llwyndafydd a Hirlas, or drinking horn, literally a 'long, blue' horn.

The Hirlas horn was tipped with silver and mounted on a silver stand on which are engraved the royal arms of England with models of the greyhound of Richmond and the Welsh dragon as supporters. This relic of Henry's march through Wales was later given to Richard Vaughan, second Earl of Carbery, who commanded the royalist forces in the area during the Civil War.[6]

Following his overnight rest at Lwyndafydd, Henry is reputed on 10

August to have stopped for the night at Wern Newydd, barely four miles from Llwyndafydd in the adjacent parish of Llanarth. But as he averaged over twenty miles a day during the march through Wales, this particular stay is unlikely.

There can be little doubt that on 10 August, camp was pitched on this night somewhere near Aberystwyth. Local tradition states that this particular stopping place was St Hilary's church at Llanilar, about four miles south of Aberystwyth. As part of this tradition, Henry is related to have slept at the old mansion of Llidiardau nearby, which overlooks the Ystwyth valley.[7]

A halt at Llanilar on the night of 10 August 1485 would have made good sense. On the next day Henry's men could have circumvented the royal castle at Aberystwyth by marching northwards through the ancient settlement of Llanbadarn. From Llanbadarn the road north leads directly to the Dovey estuary and Machynlleth. Henry did not stay here but turned eastwards towards Shrewsbury, resting for the night of 11 August at Mathafarn, the home of Dafydd Llwyd, about five miles east of Machynlleth.

Dafydd Llwyd, as we have noted, was the most prominent of the Welsh poets promoting Henry Tudor's cause. At Mathafarn, Henry is supposed, according to tradition, to have consulted with the seer over the outcome of his bid for the throne.

Specific forecasting – as opposed to general prophecy – was difficult for obvious reasons, and the seer in turn consulted his wife. She is held to have told her husband to prophesy victory for Henry of Richmond. If he failed, it was most unlikely that he would call again at Mathafarn. If he were successful, he might offer the poet a reward. This often-told legend may be a little unjust to Dafydd Llwyd in view of his passionate partisanship of the Tudor cause. But Henry's cause was indeed victorious, and Dafydd Llwyd was made an Esquire of the Body after Bosworth by Henry VII.

At about this stage of Henry's march through Wales, he sent a message to Rhys ap Thomas promising him the 'perpetual Lieutenantship' of Wales for his allegiance. Polydore Vergil leaves the impression that Henry was uncertain of Rhys's intentions during this initial stage of the march to Bosworth.

Events were soon to show, however, that Rhys must have begun his own advance towards Shrewsbury within a very short time of Henry's landing. There is no evidence that Rhys met Richmond at Dale. Rather, Rhys ap Thomas's starting place for his march north was probably Carmarthen. From here he advanced up the Tywi valley to Llandovery, and so eastwards to Brecon. These three towns are all mentioned in the family 'Life' as being on his line of march.

This family biography also states that at the beginning of his march Rhys had given orders to fire prepared warning beacons as he summoned his forces to meet him along his pre-arranged route, 'some in one place, some in another on his way to Shrewsbury . . . his snowball gathering more and more in the rolling . . .' It is recorded that at Brecon, Rhys picked up support from the Vaughan and Gam families of the March. Rhys also detached a force of cavalry from his main contingent to act as a rearguard in case of disaster.[8] In spite of the partisan origins of the 'Life', these details of Rhys's march north in support of Henry Tudor remain convincing.

From Brecon, Rhys ap Thomas and his Welsh levies struck north across the Eppynt Hills to Builth, probably the most difficult part of his march. The route northwards probably then took Rhys along the upper Wye valley to Rhayader and so across the watershed to the upper Severn valley at Llanidloes. From here the route to Newtown and Welshpool was relatively easy.

There is vivid – if a little overstated – testimony to Rhys's march through central Wales, in English ballads of the Tudor period.[9]

> Sir Rhys ap Thomas, a knight certain,
> Eight thousand spears brought he . . .
> Sir Rhys ap Thomas shall break the array
> For he will fight and never flee . . .

('The Ballad of the Lady Bessy')

> Then Sir Rhys ap Thomas drawes Wales with him,
> A worthy sight it was to see
> How the Welshmen rose wholly with him,
> And stogged them to Shrewsbury.

('The Rose of England')

Henry Enters Shrewsbury

After leaving Mathafarn on the morning of 12 August, Henry Tudor probably marched northwards to Mallwyd and then east through the pass of Bwlch-y-Fedwen to Castle Caereinon. Here, where he was within striking distance of the upper Severn valley, he spent the night of 12 August, according to tradition, at the house of Dolarddun. But a subsidiary force may have marched south-eastwards from Mathafarn to link with Rhys ap Thomas's scouts in the vicinity of Newtown.

The following day, 13 August, after spending the previous night at Dolarddun, Henry advanced six miles to Welshpool. He then went on to Long Mountain (Cefn Digoll) which overlooks the Severn opposite Welshpool.

Here Henry met Rhys ap Thomas who 'with a great bande of soldiers and with assuryd promises of loyalty yielded himself to his protection' (Polydore Vergil). Other Welsh contingents from north and north-east Wales also met Henry at Long Mountain. These included the followers of William Griffith of Penrhyn (near Bangor) and of Richard ap Howell of Mostyn in Flint. Another prominent supporter of Henry from the north was Rhys Fawr ap Meredudd of Plas Iolyn in the upper Conwy valley.[10]

Quite apart from those men who joined Henry in organized contingents, other Welsh squires had joined him on the march from all over Wales, from Carmarthenshire and Cardiganshire, from Merionethshire and Anglesey; from Glamorgan, Kidwelly, Gower and Monmouth. Many of these supporters were later awarded by grants or awards of local offices.[11] A. L. Rowse has noted that somewhere along the route to Bosworth Henry was joined by David Cecil, a young squire from the manor of Alltyrynys in the border lordship of Ewyas Lacy. He was the ancestor of William Cecil, Lord Burghley, the greatest of all the counsellors of the Tudors.[12]

Following this significant reinforcement of his army on 13 August 1485, Henry's combined forces camped for the night on Long Mountain.

On 14 August Henry's army advanced to the vicinity of Shrewsbury, first occupying Montford Bridge, about four miles west of the town, and Forton north of the Severn. These points would give the invaders a route into the Midlands if Henry's army was unable to take Shrewsbury. Messengers were sent to Shrewsbury asking for admission. But the senior magistrate, Thomas Mytton, refused entry. The town gates were closed and Henry Tudor's army remained for the night near Forton, Henry sleeping in that village.

The next day, 15 August, Thomas Mytton and his magistrates after further negotiation with Henry opened the gates of Shrewsbury. Henry's army was welcomed, and the day was spent in recruiting. In one week Henry had marched 150 miles from Dale to Shrewsbury, a march that had carried his forces close to the heart of England. The first stage of his campaign to win the crown was thus over.

Coordination of military forces was a major problem in the Wars of the Roses. But the effectiveness of Henry's planning and execution was shown by the junction of the separate forces that had joined him from both south and north Wales at Welshpool.

Moreover, the very speed of Henry's advance to Shrewsbury, and the enlistment on a considerable scale of his Welsh supporters, had inevitably put Richard III on the defensive. Charles Ross has written:

> If there was one political lesson to be learnt from the rebellions and invasions that punctuated the Wars of the Roses, it was the decisive importance of confronting risings at once and before they had time to gather strength. The longer they could remain in being, the stronger they became . . .[13]

For the success of his venture, however, it was imperative for Henry to gain the support of Thomas, Lord Stanley and Sir William Stanley. It was their forces who would decide the issue.

Between Henry Tudor's entry into Shrewsbury on 15 August and Bosworth Field on 22 August, his movements were thus dictated by his need to obtain the unequivocal support of the Stanleys. But it was only at the very last moment that the decisive, long-sought support from the Stanleys materialized.

Ambien Hill: Two Converging Armies

When Henry entered Shrewsbury on 15 August, Richard III was still at Nottingham. The news of Henry's unopposed entry into Shrewsbury would have destroyed any hopes that the King still held that the invaders could have been checked in Wales.

Lord Stanley, meanwhile, had made excuses for not obeying the King's instructions to return to Nottingham. Under interrogation, Stanley's son, Lord Strange, had confessed that Sir William Stanley was part of Henry Tudor's conspiracy. Strange maintained, however, that Lord Stanley himself was loyal to the King. But Richard immediately and formally declared Sir William Stanley a traitor.

As news reached the King that Henry's army was advancing eastwards from Shrewsbury, Richard realized that immediate action was necessary. On 19 August he left Nottingham for Leicester, a distance of about twenty-seven miles. During Sunday, 21 August, Richard's forces moved west from Leicester to Market Bosworth, about ten miles away. The king then set up camp near Sutton Cheney about two miles south of Market Bosworth. Nearby was Ambien Hill, a 400-foot high feature that dominated the area known locally as Redmore Plain.

By this time the Tudor army was also converging on a site near Ambien Hill. Henry had left Shrewsbury on 16 August and camped that night at Newport, about twenty miles away. At Newport he was joined by Gilbert Talbot with about 500 men. As the forces of both Lord Stanley and Sir William Stanley were hovering to the north of Watling Street, which was the high road to London, Henry continued his march on 17 August and entered Stafford where he met briefly with Sir William Stanley. That night Henry's army camped at Stafford.

Following his inconclusive talk with Sir William, Henry had no alternative but to continue the march on 18 August. He turned south-eastwards towards Watling Street and passing through Rugeley, camped for the night outside the walls of the small cathedral city of Lichfield. According to Polydore Vergil, there flocked to Henry's standard many supporters who hated King Richard 'worse than all men living'.

On the morning of 19 August, Henry Tudor entered Lichfield and was well received. Later that day his army left Lichfield and moved towards Tamworth where the Castle was probably surrendered that evening.

Accompanied by a small bodyguard, Henry was lost to his army on the night of 19 August, resting for the night at a small village near

Tamworth. His army may have taken some artillery from Tamworth Castle.

During 20 August, Henry moved south from Tamworth to Watling Street and then eastwards to Atherstone about fifty-five miles from Shrewsbury on the London road. Here camp was pitched for the night. Henry met with Lord Stanley and Sir William Stanley, and according to Polydore Vergil the three men planned their strategy against King Richard.

The following day, 21 August, the two armies finally converged in the vicinity of Ambien Hill, two miles south of Market Bosworth. Henry's army left Atherstone and marched along Watling Street over Witherly Bridge. His forces then turned east through an uncultivated area by Fenny Drayton and continued along the track known as Fenn Lanes. Camp was pitched for the night of 21 August on Whitemoors plain, between the villages of Shenton and Stoke Golding.

About a mile to the north lay Ambien Hill, approximately halfway between the villages of Sutton Cheney and Shenton. It was this hill that was to dominate the two-hour battle on the morrow of 22 August 1485.

'God Save King Henry'

The decision at Bosworth Field, fought on the Plain of Redmore, was a brief, barely recorded encounter that lasted for but two hours. The paradox of the battle lies in the historic consequences of such a shadowy clash of arms.

Yet all reconstructions are subject to the fact that no dependable contemporary account exists. The most reliable account is that of Polydore Vergil which was written over twenty years after the event. But Vergil talked to eye-witnesses, including the victor of Bosworth himself.

It is relevant to remember that Henry VII asked Polydore Vergil, the deputy papal collector in England, to write a history of England in 1506, that Vergil's relations with the King were cordial, and that his account of the events leading to Henry's victory were probably composed about 1512–14. This civilized Renaissance scholar, a native of Urbino, was naturalized in 1510.[14]

Given the importance of Polydore Vergil's account of the events
leading to Henry Tudor's victory at Bosworth, how may we assess his
history in general? Clearly when Polydore wrote his history, care was
necessary for obvious reasons; Henry Tudor's son was on the throne.
In any case, Polydore was quite frank in giving a favourable
explanation of the rise of the Tudors. The matter has been ably
summed up by Charles Ross in his recent biography of Richard III.
Professor Ross considers that Polydore 'was no official hack. Equally,
he could not afford to be wholly detached and impartial.' But Polydore,
who broke away from the medieval annalistic tradition to write history
as literature, always claimed to tell the truth.

The difficulties of reconstructing the Battle of Bosworth are compounded by the topographical changes in the field. In 1485 much
of the Whitemoors and Redmore Plain was unenclosed open land,
probably rough grazing. But by the late eighteenth century the
antiquary, W. Hutton, in *The Battle of Bosworth Field* (1788), noted
that land which was wild 300 years before had been drained and
cultivated.

In the nineteenth century a canal and a partly embanked railway line
were added to the battlefield, so complicating further reconstruction.
These changing topographical factors were considered in what is
probably one of the best modern accounts of Bosworth Field, that
published in 1897 by James Gairdner, the Victorian biographer of
Richard III and Henry VII.[15]

Despite all the man-made topographical changes of the last
half-millennium, however, the chief geographical feature of the
battlefield area, Ambien Hill, remains unchanged. It was on this
summit that Richard III deployed his forces on the morning of 22
August 1485. In the van was a force of archers under John Howard,
Duke of Norfolk. Behind Norfolk was the King with some of his most
reliable troops. The rear formation of the royal army was under the
command of Henry, Earl of Northumberland. But he is not mentioned
in Polydore Vergil's account as taking part in the action and his
inactivity may well have been due to treachery.

In the van of Henry Tudor's small army facing King Richard was a
force of archers under John de la Vere, Earl of Oxford and one of
Henry's most experienced commanders. On the right wing of the van
was Gilbert Talbot, and on the left, John Savage. Behind them was

Henry Tudor 'trusting to the aid of Thomas (Lord) Stanley, with one troop of horsemen and a few footmen'. Behind Henry lay the rest of his forces.

The critical deployment was that of the Stanleys, who had probably placed their men to the north of the main battlefield. The 'Stanleyans', as Polydore Vergil calls them, were probably composed of levies from Lancashire, Cheshire and north Wales. These forces were thus to the left of Henry's army and to the right of the King.

Polydore Vergil also states that the Tudor army was composed of about 5,000 men, the King's forces numbered about twice that, while the Stanleyans deployed about 3,000 men under the overall command of Sir William Stanley. There is no mention of Lord Stanley actually taking part in the fighting, so he was probably in charge of a smaller force.

Before the fighting, Henry Tudor had sent a message to Lord Stanley asking him to come and support the Tudor forces. The hardly encouraging reply was that Henry should set his own forces in order, and that Stanley would then come to him with his men well appointed. At this, Henry was vexed and appalled, 'yet without lingering' he ordered his men to begin the battle.

There was a marsh between the two armies, Polydore Vergil writes, which Henry decided to keep on his right flank to serve as a natural defence. With this feature on their right as ordered, Henry's archers now slowly advanced towards Ambien Hill. After they had passed the marsh, King Richard ordered a counter-attack. But the commander of the Tudor van, Oxford, sensibly kept his men tightly under control and ordered them not to go more than ten feet from their standards. This order at first confused the King's forces, who feared a trap, and there was a lull in the fighting. Moreover, many on the King's side were half-hearted, because they 'coveted the King dead than alive and therefore fought faintly . . .'

However, following this lull, the fighting between the two van-guards continued 'hot on both sides'. It was now that Richard III made the move that was to cost him his life.

Richard's spies had reported that Henry was 'afar off', probably slightly north of the main encounter. Evidently King Richard now decided that if Henry could be eliminated, the battle would be decided without the intervention of the Stanleys.

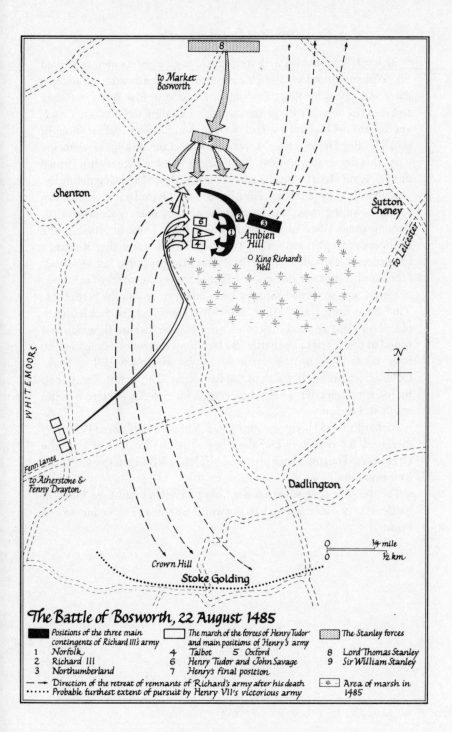

The Battle of Bosworth, 22 August 1485

| | Positions of the three main contingents of Richard III's army | | The march of the forces of Henry Tudor and main positions of Henry's army | | The Stanley forces |

1	Norfolk	4	Talbot	5	Oxford
2	Richard III	6	Henry Tudor and John Savage	8	Lord Thomas Stanley
3	Northumberland	7	Henry's final position	9	Sir William Stanley

→ Direction of the retreat of remnants of Richard's army after his death
⋯⋯ Probable furthest extent of pursuit by Henry VII's victorious army

Area of marsh in 1485

Richard, 'all inflamed with ire', cut through Henry's men and killed Sir William Brandon, the chief Tudor standard-bearer. Brandon's place was taken by Rhys Fawr ap Maredudd of Plas Iolyn.[16] Henry received the attack 'with great courage', according to Polydore Vergil, and fought off Richard's assault longer than his own soldiers thought possible. But Henry's men were 'now almost out of hope of victory'.

At this desperate moment, Sir William Stanley's forces intervened decisively on Henry's side. Richard was cut down, 'fighting manfully' in the midst of his enemies. Simultaneously, Oxford put Richard's van to flight, killing many in the chase as the royal army disintegrated. Among those killed in the fighting was John, Duke of Norfolk, the commander of Richard's van. Polydore Vergil states that Richard's forces lost 1,000 killed, while the Tudor army suffered but 100 dead. Northumberland and his son, the Earl of Surrey, were taken prisoner.

Henry was acclaimed King by his jubilant troops on the battlefield: 'God Save King Henry, God Save King Henry'. Lord Stanley then placed on Henry's head the crown belonging to Richard III which was found in the debris of the battle. By tradition, this action is supposed to have taken place on the site now known as Crown Hill at Stoke Golding, immediately south of the battlefield. The victor's army then marched to Leicester where they stayed for two days before moving south to London.

Richard's naked body was slung over a horse and taken to Leicester, displayed for two days and then buried in the local Church of the Greyfriars. The tomb later provided by Henry VII was destroyed at the Reformation.

For the first time since 1066 a king of England had been killed in battle. Henry Tudor's march to Bosworth was over. The Tudor era had begun.

10

Tudor Postscript

Henry Tudor and his advisers acted quickly to establish the new reign. On 3 September 1485 the King was received ceremonially in the City of London; and Henry proceeded to place the standards used at Bosworth in St Paul's. These standards included the Arms of St George and the 'Red Fiery Dragon' on green and white sarcenet that had been carried on the march through Wales. Prayers were offered and a *Te Deum* sung.

What sort of man was it that the victory at Bosworth had so suddenly made king, a victory that was to have such historic results? Polydore Vergil, who came to know Henry well, described Henry's appearance towards the end of his life. He wrote that

> his body was slender but well built and strong; his height above the average. His appearance was remarkably attractive and his face was cheerful, especially when speaking; his eyes were small and blue, his teeth few, poor and blackish; his hair was thin and white; his complexion sallow. His spirit was distinguished, wise and prudent; his mind was brave and resolute and never, even at moments of greatest danger, deserted him . . . In government he was shrewd and prudent, so that no one dared to get the better of him through deceit and guile . . . He was most fortunate in war, although he was constitutionally more inclined to peace than war. He cherished justice above all things; as a result he vigorously punished violence, manslaughter and every kind of violence . . . He was the most ardent supporter of our faith and daily participated with great piety in religious services . . .[1]

Polydore Vergil in these remarks also comments that 'all these virtues were obscured latterly by avarice . . .' This quality may have been a compensation for Henry's early insecurity. But many of the positive qualities noted by Polydore Vergil were echoed in Sir Francis Bacon's famous account of Henry's life and reign published in 1622. Bacon considered that Henry was 'a wonder for wise men' and such a master of affairs that 'what he minded he compassed'.[2]

Bacon's vivid portrait of Henry Tudor as the wise prince inevitably omits by its very compression some of Henry's human qualities that later scholarship has discerned. But there can be little doubt that the reign of the first Tudor was characterized by a mixture of practicality and piety, a complex fusion of the medieval and modern qualities that distinguished Henry's character. In short, he was a calculating, suspicious but effective monarch in his largely successful quest for order, stability and the founding of a dynasty.

Yet the immediate task in the aftermath of Bosworth was the consolidation of the new reign. The new King had to receive the formal sanction of Parliament. There was the promised marriage to Elizabeth of York (Edward IV's daughter) to implement the reconciliation of Lancaster and York. His followers had to be rewarded as an elementary act of self-preservation.

Accordingly, on 30 October 1485, Henry was anointed and crowned King. Parliament then met and the legal problems of the accession were solved by an Act which declared that the inheritance of the crown, 'be, rest, remain and abide in the most royal person of our now sovereign lord, King Henry VII, and in the heirs of his body lawfully coming, perpetually with the grace of God so to endure, and in none other'.[3]

By this phraseology which accepted the fact of Henry's accession, any debate over the rights and wrongs of his succession was avoided. The Act thus tacitly accepted Henry's victory at Bosworth as divine will, which put his title beyond dispute. After the passage of the Act, Henry addressed the Commons and stated that he came to the throne by just hereditary title as well as by *verum dei judicium*, the true will of God. Ever since this Act, it may be noted, the crown of England has remained vested in the heirs of Henry VII, although not through his male heirs only.

Parliament showed its concern for the establishment of the new reign by petitioning the King to marry Elizabeth of York as Henry had promised in exile. The marriage took place on 18 January 1486. The full papal dispensation, necessary as Henry and Elizabeth were of the same kinship, followed. The Papal Bull recognized both Henry's title and the validity of the marriage. It also threatened excommunication to all rebels against his rule.

The formal blessing of Church and State for Henry's accession, title, and marriage was accompanied by a widespread distribution of awards and honours to Henry's supporters.

Foremost amongst the recipients was Henry's uncle, Jasper Tudor, perhaps the man most responsible for Henry's survival during the long years of exile and also for final victory at Bosworth. He was made Duke of Bedford and justice of south Wales. The lordship of Pembroke was restored to him, and he was also given the lordships of Glamorgan, Abergavenny and Haverfordwest, as well as many of the Duchy of Lancaster revenues in Wales.

When Jasper Tudor's honours were added to the crown lands of York and Lancaster in Wales, and to the Royal Principality, it put Henry VII in a more powerful position in Wales and the Marches than any of his Yorkist predecessors.

This edifice was buttressed by a series of awards to Rhys ap Thomas. In November 1485 Sir Rhys was made chamberlain of the Royal Principality of south Wales and he was granted the offices of steward and constable of the lordship of Brecon. He was also made steward of the lordship of Builth. Rhys continued to serve actively the new King for he was present at the hard-fought Battle of Stoke in 1487, and took part in the expedition against Boulogne in 1492.

Jasper Tudor died in December 1495, and he was succeeded as justice of south Wales the following month by Rhys ap Thomas. In this way Rhys achieved a far greater measure of power and authority than Gruffydd ap Nicholas, but this power was won by loyalty, not defiance, to the crown. For all his services to Henry, Rhys ap Thomas was made in April 1505 a Knight of the Garter, the order which has been described by S. B. Chrimes as 'the ultimate mark of honour favoured by Henry VII'.

Meanwhile, the Stafford lordship of Brecon remained in the hands of the King during the minority of Edward, Duke of Buckingham. William Griffith of Penrhyn was reconfirmed as chamberlain of north Wales one month following Bosworth Field.

Many of Henry Tudor's English supporters were generously awarded. The Stanleys, who had probably decided the day at Bosworth, were given important preferment. Thomas, Lord Stanley, was made

Earl of Derby and constable of England. His younger brother, Sir William, was reconfirmed as justice of north Wales and made chamberlain of the household.

Henry Tudor's mother, Lady Margaret Beaufort, was given back lands confiscated by Richard III and also presented with many endowments to sustain her religious and educational works. She became in effect the Dowager Queen Mother. The cleric John Morton, Bishop of Ely, who had promoted Henry's cause from Brecon Castle in 1483, and had thereafter gone into exile in Flanders, was made Archbishop of Canterbury as well as Chancellor of England during 1486.

Yet it was many years before Henry's reign, let alone the dynasty, was secure. Henry and Elizabeth had eight children but three died in infancy, and of their three sons, Arthur, Edmund and Henry, only the last survived, to become Henry VIII. Two of their daughters, Margaret and Mary, survived into maturity, and it was through Margaret's marriage to James IV of Scotland that the union of the crowns came about in 1603. The death of Henry's first-born, Arthur, Prince of Wales, in 1502, was an enormous blow for the royal parents.

Moreover, to these elemental uncertainties were added the possibilities of another Bosworth mounted against Henry. Yorkist sentiment remained. It was combined with international intrigue involving France, Scotland and Burgundy in at least the early part of Henry's reign before his diplomatic talents made England an indispensable part of the European concert. The King probably never forgot that his own successful bid for the throne would not have been possible without some degree of foreign complicity.

The first (and probably the most serious) crisis of the reign revolved around the young Yorkist imposter Lambert Simnel. He was crowned 'King Edward VI' in Dublin in May 1487; the Irish lords who backed him claimed that he was Edward, Earl of Warwick, the son of Clarence, Edward IV's murdered brother. Warwick was in fact safely locked up in the Tower by Henry VII.

At the hard-fought battle of Stoke (near Newark) in June 1487 Henry's army triumphed against a force of tough German mercenaries and Irish levies backed by Burgundy and a Yorkist heir, John, Earl of Lincoln. He was the son of Elizabeth, Edward IV's sister, and John de la Pole, Duke of Suffolk.

Tudor Postscript

Lincoln was killed at Stoke, the last battle of the Wars of the Roses. But by 1491 another Yorkist imposter, Perkin Warbeck, made his appearance at Cork. He was the personable son of a Flemish tradesman, who claimed to be Richard, Duke of York, Edward IV's younger son who had disappeared into the Tower in the summer of 1483, but whose death could not be proved.

Warbeck was backed by Margaret of Burgundy, a sister of Edward IV. The Warbeck conspiracy was also supported by Sir William Stanley, who was executed for his complicity in 1495, a striking illustration of the internal security problems of Henry VII's reign.

After many adventures which must have caused great anxiety to the King, Warbeck was captured in 1497 and eventually executed in 1499. Also executed at the same time for what were really reasons of state was Edward, Earl of Warwick. Thus perished the last direct male heir of York.

Perhaps not until the imprisonment in the Tower of Lincoln's brother, Edmund, Earl of Suffolk, in 1506 was the ghost of York truly laid for Henry VII. But there was no rebellion after 1497, and the ever-increasing financial resources of the Tudor regime made successful conspiracy more remote.

Thus despite the anxieties posed by the Yorkist pretenders and many other vicissitudes inseparable from the circumstances of his accession, Henry VII ruled for twenty-four years until his death at Richmond Palace on 21 April 1509. In the same period prior to 1485 there had been four kings of England. Moreover, the royal finances were triumphantly solvent at Henry VII's death. This solvency had bought patronage and hence stability at a time when the traditional aristocracy was being fettered by Henry VII's implacable system of bonds and recognizances.

To hold the throne for so long, given the anarchic legacy of the Wars of the Roses, and moreover to leave a peaceful succession to a legitimate heir, remains a historic achievement. In this way the successful founding of the Tudor dynasty in such a violent age clearly demonstrates the complex, extraordinary qualities of the claimant who had landed in Wales in 1485.

Our story must end as it began, in Wales. What was Henry VII's policy towards the country that played such an important part both in his family fortunes and in his successful bid for the throne in 1485? What were his attitudes towards the Welsh past which was so inextricably intertwined with his own personal story?

No simple answer to these questions can be given, any more than Henry's character can be simply anatomized. We know from his privy purse expenses that he was not the morose and saturnine monarch that is sometimes depicted. He kept minstrels, trumpeters and pipers, and was also a keen sportsman and countryman.

To show his awareness of his past he kept a Welsh harpist and celebrated St David's Day. He called his first son Arthur, the supreme hero of the legends that had inspired his march through Wales. The Red Dragon of Cadwaladr which he had used for his standard became one of the supporters of the royal arms. He made an allowance of £8 a year to the Greyfriars in Carmarthen so that daily mass could be kept for his father's soul and for his own after his death. He may have instituted a commission to enquire into his Welsh origins. He certainly created a Rouge Dragon Pursuivant at the College of Arms in London, an appointment that continues to be made to this day.

Yet much of his policy in Wales and the Marches showed that hard-headed realism that was so characteristic of the man. Many of his Welsh followers in 1485 were rewarded on the local level. A typical example is Adam ap Ieuan ap Jenkin, who 'for services rendered very recently at his own costs in the King's victorious march and field' was made king's attorney for life in the counties of Carmarthen and Cardigan.

Such awards were not unprecedented in the history of the fifteenth century, and as we have seen, the Yorkist kings looked after their own in Wales and the Marches. But probably significantly greater numbers of these awards were made under the first Tudor. This was not merely gratitude for support in 1485. The Wars of the Roses had shown time after time the strategic importance of Wales and the Marches and Henry was trying to ensure that the government's authority could be enforced in this sensitive and often lawless region.

Henry also sought stability in the Welsh Marches by encouraging a system of indentures between the crown and the Marcher lords. Typical of these arrangements was the 'Indenture of the Marches' made in 1490 between Henry VII and Jasper Tudor, Duke of Bedford, as Lord of Pembroke, Newport, Glamorgan and Abergavenny. In this agreement, Jasper was bound to see that his officials in the lordships concerned closely supervised the processes of law and order.

Other agreements of this nature included one between the crown and William Herbert, Earl of Huntingdon, Lord of Gower, Chepstow, Tretower and Crickhowell. In this way the King attempted to influence the administration of justice in the March, although of course he was unable to interfere directly in the internal affairs of independent lordships.

Another way of attempting to produce order in Wales and the March was Henry's recreation of the Prince of Wales's Council, first created under Edward IV. Henry VII's son Arthur, born in September 1486, was made Prince of Wales in 1489 and by 1490 the Prince's Council was in existence.

During 1493 the Prince through his Council was given considerable judicial powers in Wales and the Marches, including the Principality. A number of Marcher lordships held by the crown were transferred to his jurisdiction, including the earldom of March, the historic agglomeration comprised of the former Yorkist and Mortimer lordships. The crown now held some fifty Marcher lordships, so making it the most powerful lord Marcher. This position was further strengthened in 1495 with the execution of Sir William Stanley which brought Bromfield and Yale and also Chirk into the royal domain.

During 1501 Prince Arthur took up residence in Ludlow Castle. Following the Prince's untimely death in April 1502, the Council continued to supervise relations between the Principality, the March and the crown lordships. The watchword was administrative efficiency. But the separate legal existence of the Marcher lordships remained, and the ultimate problem was only solved by the Act of Union in 1536. Henry's policy was thus not drastic reform – that would have been too dangerous – but to infuse existing institutions with greater authority and efficiency.

Another innovatory move made by Henry VII in Wales was the granting, towards the end of his reign, of charters to several crown communities in north and central Wales. While differing in detail, these charters were intended to remove the restrictions of the Lancastrian penal code and to relieve the situation created by the progressive breakdown of medieval institutions.

Accordingly, royal charters were granted in 1505 to Bromfield and

Yale, in 1506 to Chirk and Denbigh, in 1507 to Ceri and Cydewain and to the royal counties of Anglesey, Caernarfon and Merioneth, and in 1508 to the lordship of Ruthin. A first charter had already been granted to the men of Gwynedd in 1504.[4]

Under these charters, Welshmen could purchase land and hold office within the English boroughs and towns specified. Medieval customs and dues owing to the lord Marcher (which now meant the King) were swept away; the English law of primogeniture was henceforth applicable to the descent of land and property rather than the Welsh law of gavelkind or partible inheritance.

But true to his businessman's instincts, Henry exacted fines for granting his charters. The lordships of Ceri and Cydewain, for example, had to pay 1,600 marks for renewing concessions earlier made by Richard, Duke of York to these two members of the earldom of March.

Henry was thus insistent that the crown should be compensated for the concessions made in his charters. But of course no large-scale restructuring of the Welsh government was possible during his reign. Indeed, some of the concessions in his charters were challenged in the courts by affected English burgesses immediately prior to the King's death in 1509. But Henry's intent on at least limited reform seems clear. In a more general way the Union of 1536 seems foreshadowed by his concern for good government in Wales.

Thus although the more extreme prophecies of the poets before 1485 were hardly fulfilled by Henry VII, there was a widespread awareness of a new relationship for the better between the crown and its Welsh subjects. There was probably a decline in racial tension in Wales during Henry VII's reign, and such bards as Lewis Mon and Tudur Aled set the literary precedent for the entire Tudor period with their praise of the crown. To the bard Sion Tudur (d. 1602), Henry VII was 'the one who set us free' (*Yr un a'n rhoes ninau'n rhydd*).[5]

The new dynasty found instant favour with the ever more confident Welsh gentry, those shrewd, enterprising estate builders, the foundations of whose fortunes had already been laid in the turmoil of the fifteenth century. Henry Tudor's rule united for this aspiring class the claims of self-interest with that Welsh sentiment which had been so systematically kindled by the bards in the generation prior to 1485.

Perhaps the most remarkable contemporary illustration of the new alignment between the crown and the gentry that was to dominate Welsh life for the next four centuries was the great tournament held at Carew Castle under the auspices of Sir Rhys ap Thomas in 1506. This was the last great medieval tournament of its kind to be held in Wales, a celebration from an age that was already passing.

The tournament was held to celebrate the admission of Sir Rhys ap Thomas to the Order of the Garter in 1505. He had transformed Carew Castle from a medieval fortress on an inlet of Milford Haven near Pembroke to a sophisticated mansion; the arms of Henry VII and his son Arthur can still be seen above the ruined entrance to the Great Hall.

Altogether, 1,000 persons of rank from all over Wales attended the festivities, the jousting and the feasting which lasted five days. At the head of the great banqueting table was a vacant chair for the King. Over the entrance to Carew Castle was erected a picture of St George and St David embracing each other, striking evidence of the reconciliation of interests and attitudes brought about in Wales by Henry Tudor's victory.[6]

This alliance between the Tudors and the Welsh gentry, which was to lie at the heart of the dynasty's policy in Wales, was later invoked by George Owen of Henllys. He remains perhaps the most fluent representative of this class, and probably the most talented. Writing in the last decade of Elizabeth Tudor's reign, he wrote that Henry VII was 'a Moses that delivered us from bondage', a second Solomon who 'so drew the hearts of Welshmen to him as the Lodestone doth the iron, who ever since have borne such natural love and affection' to Henry and his royal successors. George Owen went on to write that as a result of Tudor policy 'there hath not been found in England any country or province more obedient in heart than this country of Wales'.

This feeling was not merely sentiment. George Owen noted also that while earlier kings had sought the 'subversion, ruin, and impoverishing' of Wales, Henry VII and his son had come to end grievances and 'to establish good and wholesome laws among them and to give them magistrates of their choosing . . .' This was a reference to the arrangements of Henry VIII's Act of Union of 1536 which extended 'all and singular freedoms, liberties, rights, privileges and laws' of England to Wales.[7]

These were not words of merely formal obeisance to the Tudor mystique in Wales. It has been noted that as a result of Welsh devotion to Henry VII and his successors, no Yorkist pretender found any sympathy there.

Moreover, while there were rebellions in Cornwall, the North and Ireland during the early Tudor period, Wales remained quiet as a result of the alliance between the dynasty and the hard-headed and intensely loyal Welsh gentry exemplified by George Owen: 'Order, stability, prosperity, and influence were becoming synonomous in their minds with being *en rapport* with the King . . .'[8] As a result of Bosworth Field, the Tudor peace was thus both a psychological and a political reality in Wales.

A few years after Bosworth, Lewis Glyn Cothi was able to write that 'the boar is cold in his grave; the world is still, and envenomed feuds asleep'.

But the longer-term legacy of Bosworth Field was the reconciliation of Wales and England, and this transcended the immediate politics of the Tudor age.

The evident enthusiasm for Henry Tudor on the part of his Welsh subjects was reciprocated by the King. This feeling on Henry's part was distinct from the politic considerations of government in Wales that we have noted above. In their astute, cautious way these reforms were of a piece with the other measured, calculating policies of early Tudor statecraft.

But there was another side to Henry's complex personality, one that reacted emotionally to the prophecies and the invocations of the British past that presaged his march through Wales to Bosworth in 1485. Henry may well have believed in some part of his mind that he was indeed the Son of Prophecy. But this belief was always kept subordinate to the demands of statecraft.

The historian, Christopher Morris, has noted that Henry Tudor

seems to have had a love for all the pageantry and panoply of an outworn and fast-fading chivalric civilization. The architectural memorials he left behind him are a blaze of heraldry. He held tournaments and indulged in pomps and 'progresses' that were labyrinths of intricate and elaborate allegory and symbolism . . .[9]

Henry, it should be remembered, had probably spent fourteen of his first twenty-eight years in Wales. Another four years had been spent in Brittany and France, where, as in Wales, Arthurian influences were prevalent. In exile, Henry had promised to marry Elizabeth of York if his bid for the throne was successful. Following Bosworth, the marriage took place and it was clearly Henry's objective to 'unite the White Rose and the Red', as Shakespeare's Richmond declaims. But Henry was to see to it that this dynastic marriage was celebrated in a way that invoked a potent political symbolism.

There was no Red Rose of Lancaster during the Wars of the Roses – the White Rose was one of Edward IV's badges – and it was probably Henry VII who invented the symbolic device of the Tudor Double Rose. The Red Rose of Lancaster was now fused with the White Rose of York. Thus was created the great Tudor myth which symbolized the Union of York and Lancaster and the healing of the national schism of the civil wars. The idea of the Tudor dynasty as an arbiter against renewed fratricidal strife quickly took hold, the Double Rose appeared in art, architecture and manuscript, and through the Tudor chroniclers the concept passed into literature. Above all the idea infused Shakespeare's tetralogy on the Wars of the Roses which influences our perception of these events to this day.

The Tudor Double Rose was thus a potent and lasting illustration of Henry Tudor's love of symbolism. But in addition to the invention of the Double Rose, Henry blazoned the Welsh Dragon in a number of significant ways. For Henry, the Dragon was evidently a symbol of his ancient Trojan descent which gave him and his dynasty a legitimacy quite distinct from the claims of York and Lancaster.

This symbolism is evident in the supporters of the royal arms of the Tudors, initiated by Henry, for the Greyhound of Richmond and Lancaster is balanced by the Dragon of Wales and Cadwaladr. Here was a symmetry which went to the deepest roots of the dynasty. It also added to the vision of the Tudors as the healers of civil war the special role of a dynasty which reconciled Wales and England after 1,000 years of conflict.

Although the dynasty's interest in their British past declined after its founder's reign, contemporaries could be in no doubt of Henry Tudor's interest in and even fascination with the symbols of his Welsh ancestry. One notable illustration of this fact was the history of

Henry's reign by the cleric Bernard André, virtually the official court historian.

This account begins with an outline of Henry's royal descent, from Cadwaladr on his father's side, and from John of Gaunt on his mother's side. The history stated explicitly that the ancient prophecies to Cadwaladr, in Geoffrey of Monmouth's *British History*, had been fulfilled in the person of Henry VII.[10]

This great theme of the family origins was given a personal emphasis by Henry VII. He named his first son Arthur, assiduously trained him to be king, and during 1501 sent him to Ludlow to govern Wales and the Marches.

Henry had arranged for his son to be born at Winchester. The city was known for its Arthurian associations which included the Round Table preserved in the Great Hall of Winchester Castle. But Arthur died in April 1502 and the reign of the Tudor King Arthur never materialized as Henry had wished.

After Prince Arthur's premature death, Henry Tudor did carry through almost to completion two architectural shrines to the dynasty. These buildings commemorate his love of symbolism and still remain as great monuments to his reign.

The first of these is the Chapel of King's College, Cambridge. The beginnings were made under Henry VI and little progress followed after his death in 1471. Under Henry VII most of the Chapel, including the vault, was built. The Chapel was then finally completed in 1515 by Henry VIII.

In the Chapel, the emblems of the Tudor Double Rose and the Beaufort Portcullis are prominent, and 'the Dragon prances in all the sculptured heraldry':

> It glows in the highest and most central place of all, in the stupendous eastern window just above the head of the crucified saviour. The founder, King Henry VI, had left instructions that the Chapel furnishings should be of an austere and simple piety. Henry VII and Henry VIII made the Chapel highly secular and highly ornate. They made it a shrine not of our lady but of 'the Tudor myth'. But the Dragons are as prominent as the Roses and show that the myth was largely a Welsh myth . . .[11]

The second great Tudor shrine is the Henry VII Chapel at the eastern end of Westminster Abbey, Henry Tudor's most memorable foundation which was almost completed in his lifetime. This 'was to be the last resting place of himself and his only queen, the monument and symbol of his life's work'.[12]

To complete the tomb, Henry's executors invited to England the Florentine Pietro Torrigiano; the austere gilt-bronze effigies of Henry and Elizabeth remain as one of the first and finest Renaissance monuments in England. In the intimate surroundings of the tomb, Henry's love of Tudor symbolism is carefully and precisely represented. The black marble tomb, completed in 1517–18, is enclosed by a bronze screen, and here a Flemish craftsman fashioned figures of the Greyhound and the Dragon. Directly above, a sculptured Dragon on one of the corbels of the chapel overlooks the tomb.

This great Chapel is thus the true memorial to Bosworth Field. But there are still some monuments in Wales to the events that culminated in the Battle of Bosworth and to the people who made Henry's victory possible.

Henry Tudor's father, Edmund Tudor, was buried in the Church of the Greyfriars, Carmarthen, following his death in 1456. After the suppression of the Greyfriars in 1538, Edmund's tomb was moved to St David's Cathedral, and now stands in the presbytery of that ancient building. The Latin inscription on the tomb calls upon the observer to notice that since even Edmund Tudor, so great a man, and so brave a warrior, had to die, so also must lesser mortals.

After Bosworth Field, Edmund's brother, Jasper Tudor, as Lord of Glamorgan, is reputed by tradition to have built the north-west tower of Llandaff Cathedral, still known as Jasper's Tower. Following his death in 1495, Jasper was buried at Keynsham Abbey, near Bristol. But the massive town walls of Tenby still remind us of Jasper's activities in the Lancastrian cause in west Wales.

Thomas White, the mayor and merchant of Tenby who helped Henry and Jasper to escape to the Continent in 1471, is commemorated by a fine alabaster tomb in St Mary's Church, Tenby. The features on the effigy, though worn, are still discernible.

Sir Rhys ap Thomas, who died in 1525, was buried like Edmund Tudor in the Greyfriars, Carmarthen. After the dissolution, the tomb was moved to St Peter's Church at the opposite end of the town. The tomb, now much restored, stands in the aisle of St Peter's; the three ravens of Sir Rhys's arms are still visible on the splendid effigy.[13]

Relatively long sectors of Henry Tudor's road to Bosworth have escaped despoliation despite the passage of 500 years. In recent years a new lighthouse has been built on St Ann's Head, Pembrokeshire, near Mill Bay where Henry landed on 7 August 1485. But the bay itself remains a secluded cove, not easy to find, and a track still leads north to Brunt Farm and Dale.

On the Preseli Hills, Henry's resting place at Fagwr Lwyd is a heap of stones, but the site is marked by a large clump of beech trees. Further north at Llwyndafydd (near Newquay) and at Mathafarn (near Machynlleth), where Henry communed with the seer Dafydd Llwyd, his resting places have become sturdy farmhouses.

At Bosworth Field, a museum of the battle has been built in recent years near Ambien Hill, site of Richard III's last charge. Access to the area has been opened up, so giving a better appreciation of the historic battlefield than has been possible for many years.

Many of the small towns that Henry Tudor passed through in 1485 from Haverfordwest onwards have presumably changed beyond recognition. But in the Preseli Hills of Pembrokeshire and on the way through the Cambrian mountains to Shrewsbury, the road to Bosworth probably remains very much as it was in Henry's time.

Notes

Introduction

1. G. M. Trevelyan, *History of England*, Longmans Green, 1945 edn, p. 266.
2. S. B. Chrimes, *Henry VII*, Eyre Methuen, 1972, p. 3.
3. T. D. Kendrick, *British Antiquity*, Methuen, 1950, brings out the continuing influence of Geoffrey's *British History* in Tudor times.

The Great Rebellion

1. M. E. Griffiths, *Early Vaticination in Welsh with English Parallels*, University of Wales Press, 1937.
2. A. G. Bradley, *Owen Glyndwr*, Putnam, 1902, pp. 266–8.
3. R. R. Davies, 'Owain Glyn Dwr and the Welsh Squirearchy', *Trans. Hon. Soc. of Cymmrodorion*, 1968, pp. 152, 162, 168.
4. J. E. Lloyd, *Owen Glendower*, Oxford University Press, 1931, p. 93.
5. Glanmor Williams, *Owen Glendower*, Oxford University Press, 1966, pp. 59–60. I have quoted from Geoffrey of Monmouth, *The History of the Kings of Britain*, trans. Lewis Thorpe, Penguin, 1966.

The Silent Revolution

1. Howell T. Evans, *Wales and the Wars of the Roses*, Cambridge University Press, 1915, p. 47.
2. Glyn Roberts, 'The Threshold of the Modern Age', in *Aspects of Welsh History*, University of Wales Press, 1969, p. 290.
3. J. R. Lander, *The Wars of the Roses*, Secker & Warburg, 1966, p. 29.
4. Ralph A. Griffiths, 'Gentlemen and Rebels in Later Medieval Cardiganshire', *Ceredigion: Journal of the Cardiganshire Antiquarian*

Notes

Society, vol. V, 1965, p. 158. For the cancelling of the great sessions, T. B. Pugh, *The Marcher Lordships of South Wales: 1415–1536*, University of Wales Press, 1963, pp. 36–43.

5. Evans, *Wales and the Wars of the Roses*, p. 42; Sir John Wynn, *The History of the Gwydir Family*, University of Wales Press, 1927, pp. 38–9.

6. Glanmor Williams, *The Welsh Church from Conquest to Reformation*, University of Wales Press, 1976 edn, pp. 251–3.

7. Glyn Roberts, 'Wales and England: Antipathy and Sympathy 1282–1485', *Aspects of Welsh History*, p. 317; *A Dictionary of Welsh Biography Down to 1940*, Hon. Soc. of Cymmrodorion, London, 1959, pp. 180–1. Cited as *DWB*.

8. Francis Jones, 'Sir Rhys ap Thomas', *Transactions of the Carmarthenshire Antiquarian Society and Field Club*, vol. 29, 1939.

9. Ralph A. Griffiths, 'Gruffydd ap Nicholas and the Rise of the House of Dinefwr', *National Library of Wales Journal*, vol. 13, no. 3, 1964, pp. 259–60; for the later phases of Gruffydd's career, *idem*, 'Gruffydd ap Nicholas and the Fall of the House of Lancaster', *Welsh History Review*, vol. 2, no. 3, 1965.

10. 'The Life of Rhys ap Thomas', *Cambrian Register*, I, 1795, p. 57. For further details of this family history, see Chapter 8 below.

The House of Tudor

1. *DWB*, pp. 180–1. For the rulers of Deheubarth (south Wales) and Gwynedd (north Wales) see Sir J. E. Lloyd, *History of Wales from the Earliest Times to the Edwardian Conquest*, Longmans, 1939 edn, pp 764–9. Both lines had a common ancestor in Rhodri the Great.

2. Glyn Roberts, 'Wyrion Eden: The Anglesey Descendants of Ednyfed Fychan in the Fourteenth Century', *Aspects of Welsh History*, 1969. The article was originally published in *Trans. of the Anglesey Antiq. Soc.* (1951).

3. Royal Commission on Ancient and Historical Monuments in Wales and Mon., *Anglesey Inventory*, HMSO, 1937, pp. cxxxvii–viii, pp. 129–30, and plates 85 and 86. The *Inventory* describes Goronwy's tomb as 'one of the most costly monuments of the type fashionable in England in the period about 1380–90'. The assigned arms of the chieftain Marchudd, ancestor of the Tudors, comprised a giant's head erased at the neck, which Ednyfed Fychan is said to have changed for three Englishmen's heads. The heads were later changed to helmets, according to one story. See Francis Jones, *The Princes and Principality of Wales*, University of Wales Press, 1969, pp. 172–3.

4. R. R. Davies, 'Owain Glyn Dwr and the Welsh Squirearchy', *THS*, 1968, p. 154.

5. J. E. Lloyd, *Owen Glendower*, p. 91.

6. Roberts, 'Wyrion Eden', pp. 203–4.

7. Chrimes, *Henry VII*, p. 6.

8. Polydore Vergil, *Three Books of English History*, ed. Sir H. Ellis, Camden Soc., old series, vol. 29, 1844, p. 62. Cited as 'Polydore Vergil'. The translation of this edition dates from the mid-sixteenth century.

9. Chrimes, *Henry VII*, pp. 8–13; *DWB*, s.n. Owain, Edmund, and Jasper Tudor. For further details on the career of Owain, his two sons, and Henry Tudor, cf. Roger S. Thomas, 'The political career, estates and connection of Jasper Tudor, Earl of Richmond and Duke of Bedford, d. 1495', unpublished University of Wales Ph.D. dissertation, 1971.

War in Wales

1. G. M. Trevelyan, *History of England*, Longmans Green, 1945 edn, p. 213.

2. Charles Ross, *The Wars of the Roses*, Thames & Hudson, 1976, pp. 31–2.

3. Ralph A. Griffiths, 'Gruffydd ap Nicholas and the Fall of the House of Lancaster', *Welsh History Review*, vol. 2, no. 3, 1965, pp. 223–4.

4. J. Gairdner (ed.), *The Paston Letters*, vol. I, London, 1901 edn, p . 392.

5. Griffiths, 'Gruffyd ap Nicholas and the Fall of the House of Lancaster', p. 225; R. L. Storey, *The End of the House of Lancaster*, Barrie & Rockliffe, London, 1966, pp. 179–80.

6. Evans, *Wales and the Wars of the Roses*, pp. 95–6.

7. R. F. Walker, 'Jasper Tudor and the Town of Tenby', *National Library of Wales Journal*, vol. 16, no. 1, Summer 1969, p. 4.

8. Ross, *The Wars of the Roses*, p. 37.

9. Evans, *Wales and the Wars of the Roses*, p. 126; Anthony Goodman, *The Wars of the Roses*, Routledge & Kegan Paul, 1981, pp. 49–50.

10. J. Gairdner (ed.), 'Gregory's Chronicle', in *The Historical Collections of a Citizen of London*, Camden Society, new series, No. 27, 1876, p. 211.

11. Ross, *The Wars of the Roses*, p. 54. Cf. the same author's *Edward IV*, Eyre Methuen, 1974, for a comprehensive account of the Yorkist era.

Yorkist Victory

1. Evans, *Wales and the Wars of the Roses*, p. 141.

2. T. B. Pugh (ed.), *Glamorgan Co. History*, vol. III, 1971, pp. 258–9. Philip Mansel's lands were restored to his heir, Jenkin Mansel, by Henry VII's first parliament.

3. J. M. Lewis, *Carreg Cennen Castle*, DOE Guidebook, 1972.

Notes

4. Chrimes, *Henry VII*, pp. 15–17.
5. *Glamorgan Co. History*, vol. III, p. 260.
6. Evans, *Wales and the Wars of the Roses*, p. 171.
7. *Ibid.*, p. 185. For Sir Thomas ap Roger Vaughan's career, *DWB*, p. 997.
8. Polydore Vergil, *Three Books of English History*, pp. 134–5.
9. *Ibid.*, pp. 154–5; for a sometimes romantic account of these events with many details of the Tudor connection with Pembrokeshire, cf. W. Done Bushell, 'The Lady Margaret Beaufort and King Henry VII', *Archaeologia Cambrensis*, 1916, pp. 189–221, 301–40.

Henry Tudor's Exile

1. Penry Williams, *The Council in the Marches of Wales under Elizabeth I*, University of Wales Press, 1958, Chapter I.
2. There is a detailed account of these events in E. F. Jacob, *The Fifteenth Century, 1399–1485*, Oxford History of England, 1961. Cf. Charles Ross, *Richard III*, Eyre Methuen, 1981.
3. Chrimes, *Henry VII*, pp. 31–2. Appendix B lists 'Henry of Richmond's companions in exile, 1483–85'.
4. Evans, *Wales and the Wars of the Roses*, p. 214.
5. *Glamorgan Co. History*, vol. III, p. 263. Annuities of £152 from the counties of Carmarthen and Cardigan, and the lordship of Haverfordwest, were assigned to the Earl and Countess by Richard III.
6. Wynn, *The History of the Gwydir Family*, 1927, pp. 27–8. Sir John Wynn was a descendant of John ap Maredudd.

Prophecy and Politics

1. Thomas Parry, *History of Welsh Literature*, trans. H. I. Bell, Oxford University Press, 1955, pp. 26–7. For a full description of the prophetic material in Welsh, cf. M. E. Griffiths, *Early Vaticination in Welsh with English Parallels*, University of Wales Press, 1937.
2. W. Garmon Jones, 'Welsh Nationalism and Henry Tudor', *Trans. Hon. Soc. of Cymmrodorion*, 1917–18, p. 9.
3. The social role of the bards is described in Gwyn Williams, *An Introduction to Welsh Poetry*, Faber and Faber, 1953, pp. 7–12.
4. Garmon Jones, 'Welsh Nationalism and Henry Tudor', pp. 14–15.
5. For Owain Lawgoch (Owain ap Thomas ap Rhodri) see *DWB*, p. 690.
6. Evan D. Jones, 'Wales in Fifteenth Century Politics', *Wales Through the Ages*, vol. 1, Christopher Davies, 1975 edn, p. 185.

7. Parry, History of Welsh Literature, pp. 158–9.

8. Evans, *Wales and the Wars of the Roses*, pp. 10–11, 93–4; *DWB*, pp. 544–5; the ode to Gruffydd ap Nicholas is in J. Jones and W. Davies, *The Poetical Works of Lewis Glyn Cothi*, vol. 1, Oxford, 1837, pp. 131–7.

9. *DWB*, p. 322; Evans, *Wales and the Wars of the Roses*, pp. 170–1, 185.

10. W. Garmon Jones, 'Welsh Nationalism and Henry Tudor', p. 24.

11. *DWB*, p. 102.

12. Glanmor Williams, 'Prophecy, Politics and Poetry in Medieval and Tudor Wales', in H. Hearder and H. R. Loyn (eds.), *British Government and Administration: Essays Presented to S. B. Chrimes*, University of Wales Press, 1974, p. 114.

For a Welsh edition of Dafydd Llwyd's works containing several poems to Henry Tudor, cf. W. R. Richards, *Gwaith Dafydd Llwyd o Fathafarn*, University of Wales Press, 1964.

13. A. H. Dodd, 'Nationalism in Wales: A Historical Assessment', *Trans. Hon. Soc. of Cymmrodorion*, 1970, p. 42; Jones, 'Wales in Fifteenth Century Politics', p. 191.

14. Williams, 'Prophecy, Politics and Poetry in Medieval and Tudor Wales', pp. 115–16.

15. Jones, 'Welsh Nationalism and Henry Tudor', pp. 40, 18. For further details on the prophetic poetry, cf. C. H. Thomas, 'The Political History of Wales from 1350–1485 as reflected in the literature of the period', unpublished University of Wales M.A. dissertation, 1936.

Henry's Welsh Ally

1. *DWB*, p. 313, s.n. Gruffydd ap Nicholas.

2. Francis Jones, 'Abermarlais', *Archaeologia Cambrensis*, 1967, p. 168.

3. *Ibid.*

4. *DWB*, pp. 840–1, s.n. Rhys ap Thomas.

5. Francis Jones, 'Sir Rhys ap Thomas', *Trans. Carms. Antiq. Soc.*, 1939, p. 32. For further details on Sir Rhys's career, cf. the articles on him in the *Arch. Camb.* for 1878 and 1892 by H. W. Lloyd and David Jones respectively.

6. 'The Life of Rhys ap Thomas: A short view of the long life of the ever-wise, valiant and fortunate commander, Rhys ap Thomas, Knight, Constable, and Lieutenant of Brecknock', *Cambrian Register*, vol. I, 1795. The late Glyn Roberts, *DWB*, p. 847, considered that Henry Rice was 'certainly' the anonymous author.

7. Ralph A. Griffiths, 'Gentlemen and Rebels in Later Medieval Cardiganshire', *Ceredigion*, 1965, pp. 159–60.

Notes

For further details of Sir Rhys's career, see J. M. Lloyd, 'The Rise and Fall of the House of Dinefwr (the Rhys family) 1430–1530', unpublished University of Wales M.A.dissertation, 1963.

The Road to Bosworth

1. George Owen, *The Description of Pembrokeshire*, ed. Henry Owen, Part I, Cymmrodorion Record Series, 1892, p. 262; Edward Laws, *The History of Little England Beyond Wales*, Bell, 1888, p. 222; H. Thornhill Timmins, *Nooks and Corners of Pembrokeshire*, Elliot Stock, 1895, pp. 123–4.

2. S. B. Chrimes, 'The Landing Place of Henry of Richmond, 1485', *Welsh History Review*, vol. II, no 2, 1964, pp. 178–9.

3. Evans, *Wales and the Wars of the Roses*, p. 219. The elaborate preparations of Pembroke Castle are described by this writer on p. 214.

4. Chrimes, 'The Landing Place of Henry of Richmond, 1485', pp. 176–7.

5. I have followed W. Tom Williams, 'Henry of Richmond's Itinerary to Bosworth', *Y Cymmrodor*, vol. 29, 1919, for the details of Henry's march and his overnight stops. Cf. the reconstruction in William Rees, *An Historical Atlas of Wales*, Faber and Faber, 1959 edn, plate 54. Lander, *Wars of the Roses*, Chapter 6, prints the relevant passages from the Croyland chronicle.

6. In addition to Tom Williams' article above, for the stay at Llwyndafydd see S. R. Meyrick (ed.), *The Heraldic Visitations of Lewis Dwnn*, vol. I, 1846, p. 80. An engraving of the Hirlas horn forms the frontispiece to this work. The Hirlas horn passed from the Vaughans of Golden Grove to the ancestors of the present Lord Cawdor.

7. For this tradition, see the *Western Mail*, Cardiff, 8 June 1982.

8. 'The Life of Rhys ap Thomas', pp. 105–6.

9. Evans, *Wales and the Wars of the Roses*, pp. 223–4.

10. Emyr Wyn Jones, 'Wales and Bosworth Field: Selective Historiography?' *National Library of Wales Journal*, vol. 21, no. 1, Summer 1979, pp. 48–50.

11. Evans, *Wales and the Wars of the Roses*, pp. 224–7.

12. A. L. Rowse, 'Alltyrynys and the Cecils', *English Historical Review*, 1960.

13. Ross, *The Wars of the Roses*, p. 89. Cf. Albert Makison, 'The Road to Bosworth Field, August 1485', *History Today*, vol. 13, 1963, pp. 239–49.

14. Polydore Vergil, p. vii.

15. J. Gairdner, 'The Battle of Bosworth', *Archaeologia*, second series, vol. LV, 1896, pp. 158–78. This article contains a particularly clear map of the battlefield facing p. 178. Gairdner concluded his article by writing that 'the

Notes

whole conflict had lasted little more than two hours. But in those two hours the reign of feudal disorder had come to an end and a foundation had been laid for firm and consistent government.'

16. J. Y. W. Lloyd, *A History of Powys Fadog*, vol. III, 1882, pp. 341–2.

Tudor Postscript

1. *The Anglica Historia of Polydore Vergil 1485–1537*, D. Hay, Camden Society, new series, vol. 74, 1950, pp. 145–7.

2. Francis Bacon, *The History of King Henry VII*, Works, ed. J. A. Spedding *et al.*, vol. VI, 1878, pp. 238–44.

3. Details in Chrimes, *Henry VII*, Chapter 2.

4. J. Beverley Smith, 'Crown and Community in the Principality of North Wales in the Reign of Henry Tudor', *Welsh History Review*, vol. 3, no. 2, 1966.

5. R. R. Davies, 'The Twilight of Welsh Law, 1284–1536', *History*, vol. 51, 1966, p. 153.

6. For the Carew Castle tournament, see Richard Fenton, *Historical Tour Through Pembrokeshire*, 1811 and Edward Laws, *The History of Little England Beyond Wales*, 1888.

7. George Owen, *A description of Pembrokeshire*, Part III, 1906, pp. 37–8, 55. The words quoted are from Owen's treatise, 'The Dialogue of the Government of Wales'; according to B. G. Charles, *George Owen of Henllys: A Welsh Elizabethan*, NLW, 1973, p. 137, the Treatise is an 'enconium of the manifold blessings bestowed by the Tudors on the country of their origin'.

8. Glanmor Williams, *The Welsh Church from Conquest to Reformation*, pp. 554, 557–8.

9. Christopher Morris, *The Tudors*, Batsford, 1955, p. 59.

10. Sydney Anglo, 'The *British History* in Early Tudor Propaganda', *Bulletin of the John Rylands Library*, vol. 44, 1961, p. 24. The reference to Henry's origins is from Bernard André's *Historia Regis Henrici Septimi*, in J. Gairdner (ed.), *Memorials of King Henry VII*, Rolls Series, London, 1858, pp. 9–11.

11. Morris, *The Tudors*, p. 60.

12. Chrimes, *Henry VII*, p. 305.

13. Following the execution of Sir Rhys ap Thomas's grandson, Rhys ap Gruffydd, for treason in 1531, the family estates were forfeited to the crown. 'The next three generations of the family attempted to rebuild the family fortunes, and they succeeded in regaining some of the forfeited lands, though by far the greater part was disposed of by successive Tudor monarchs.' *DWB*, p. 847.

Select Bibliography

Anglo, Sydney, 'The *British History* in Early Tudor Propaganda', *Bulletin of the John Rylands Library*, vol. 44, 1961.

Bradley, A. G., *Owen Glyndwr*, Putnam, 1902.

Charles, B. G., *George Owen of Henllys*, National Library of Wales, 1973.

Chrimes, S. B., *Henry VII*, Eyre Methuen, 1972.

    'The Landing Place of Henry of Richmond, 1485', *Welsh History Review*, vol. 2, no. 2, 1964.

    'The Reign of Henry VII: Some Recent Contributions', *Welsh History Review*, vol. 10, no. 3, 1981.

Davies, R. R., *Lordship and Society in the March of Wales, 1282–1400*, Oxford University Press, 1978.

    'Owain Glyn Dŵr and the Welsh Squirearchy', Trans. Hon. Soc. of Cymmrodorion, 1968.

    'The Twilight of Welsh Law', *History*, vol. 51, 1966.

Dictionary of Welsh Biography Down to 1940, Trans. Hon. Soc. of Cymmrodorion, 1959.

Dodd, A. H., 'Nationalism in Wales: A Historical Assessment', *Trans. Hon. Soc. of Cymmrodorion*, 1970.

Done Bushell, W., 'The Lady Margaret Beaufort and King Henry VII', *Archaeologia Cambrensis*, 1916.

Evans, Howell T., *Wales and the Wars of the Roses*, Cambridge University Press, 1915.

Gairdner, J., *Memorials of King Henry VII*, Rolls Series, London, 1858.

    'The Historical Collections of a Citizen of London', Camden Soc., new series, no. 17, 1876.

    'The Battle of Bosworth', *Archaeologia*, vol. LV, 1896.

Goodman, Anthony, *The Wars of the Roses*, Routledge & Kegan Paul, 1981.

Griffiths, M. E., *Early Vaticination in Welsh with English Parallels*, University of Wales Press, 1937.

Griffiths, Ralph A., *The Reign of Henry VI*, Benn, 1981.

    'Gruffydd ap Nicholas and the Rise of the House of Dinefwr', *National Library of Wales Journal*, vol. 13, no. 3, 1964.

Select Bibliography

'Gruffydd ap Nicholas and the Fall of the House of Lancaster', *Welsh History Review*, vol. 2, no. 3, 1965.

'Gentlemen and Rebels in Later Medieval Cardiganshire', *Ceredigion: Journal of the Cardiganshire Antiquarian Soc.*, 1965.

'Wales and the Marches', in *Fifteenth Century England 1399–1509: Studies in Politics and Society*, ed. S. B. Chrimes, C. D. Ross and R. A. Griffiths, Manchester University Press, 1972.

Jacob, E. F., *The Fifteenth Century*, Oxford University Press, 1961.

Jerman, H. N., 'A Map of the Routes of Henry Tudor and Rhys ap Thomas Through Wales in 1485', *Archaeologia Cambrensis*, 1937.

Jones, E. D., 'Wales in Fifteenth Century Politics', *Wales Through the Ages*, vol. 1, Christopher Davies, 1975 edn.

Jones, Emyr Wyn, 'Wales and Bosworth Field: Selective Historiography', *National Library of Wales Journal*, vol. 21, no. 1, 1979.

Jones, Francis, *The Princes and Principality of Wales*, University of Wales Press, 1969.

'Sir Rhys ap Thomas', *Trans. of the Carmarthenshire Antiquarian Soc.*, vol. 29, 1939.

'Abermarlais', *Archaeologia Cambrensis*, 1967.

Jones, W. Garmon, 'Welsh Nationalism and Henry Tudor', *Trans. Hon. Soc. of Cymmrodorion*, 1917–18.

Jones, J. and Davies, W., *Poetical Works of Lewis Glyn Cothi*, 2 vols., Oxford, 1837.

Kendrick, T. D., *British Antiquity*, Methuen, 1950.

Lander, J. R., *The Wars of the Roses*, Secker & Warburg, 1965.

Laws, Edward, *The History of Little England Beyond Wales*, Bell, 1888.

Lewis, J. M., *Carreg Cennen Castle*, DOE Handbook, 1972.

Lloyd, J. E., *Owen Glendower*, Oxford University Press, 1931.

History of Wales, 2 vols., Longmans, 1939 edn.

Lloyd, J. M., 'The Rise and Fall of the House of Dinefwr (the Rhys family) 1430–1530', unpublished University of Wales M.A. dissertation, 1963. Copy available in National Library of Wales.

'The Life of Rhys ap Thomas', *Cambrian Register*, I, 1795.

Makison, Albert, 'The Road to Bosworth Field, August 1485', *History Today*, vol. 13, 1963.

McFarlane, K. B., 'The Wars of the Roses', *Proceedings of the British Academy*, vol. 50, 1964.

Meyrick, S. R. (ed.), *The Heraldic Visitations of Lewis Dwnn*, 2 vols., Llandovery, 1846.

Morris, Christopher, *The Tudors*, Batsford, 1955.

Owen, George, *The Description of Pembrokeshire*, ed. Henry Owen, Cymmrodorion Record Series, I., London, 1892–1936. (Four vols.)

Select Bibliography

Parry, Thomas, *History of Welsh Literature*, trans. H. I. Bell, Oxford
University Press, 1955.

Pugh, T. B., *The Marcher Lordships of South Wales, 1415–1536*, University of
Wales Press, 1963.

    (ed.) *Glamorgan County History, Vol. III: The Middle Ages*, Cardiff,
1971.

    'The Magnates, Knights and Gentry', in *Fifteenth Century England*
(above).

Rees, William, *An Historical Atlas of Wales*, Faber and Faber, 1959
edn.

Richards, W. L., *Gwaith Dafydd Llwyd o Fathafarn*, University of Wales
Press, 1964.

Roberts, Glyn, *Aspects of Welsh History*, University of Wales Press, 1969.

    'Wales and England: Antipathy and Sympathy, 1282–1485', *Welsh
History Review*, vol. 1, no. 4, 1963. Reprinted in *Aspects of Welsh
History*.

Ross, Charles, *Edward IV*, Eyre Methuen, 1974.

    The Wars of the Roses, Eyre Methuen, 1976.

    Richard III, Eyre Methuen, 1981.

Rowse, A. L., *Bosworth Field and the Wars of the Roses*, Macmillan, 1966.

    'Alltyrynys and the Cecils', *English Historical Review*, vol. 74, 1960.

Royal Commission on Ancient and Historical Monuments in Wales & Mon.

    Carmarthenshire Inventory, 1917. S.n., St Peter's Church, Carmarthen,
Tomb of Rhys ap Thomas.

    Pembrokeshire Inventory, 1925. S.n., St David's Cathedral, Tomb of
Edmund Tudor.

    Anglesey Inventory, 1937. S.n., Penmynydd Church, Tomb of Goronwy
ap Tudur.

Skeel, C. A. J., 'Wales Under Henry VIII' in *Tudor Studies*, ed. R. W.
Seton-Watson, University of London Press, 1924.

Smith, J. Beverley, 'Crown and Community in the Principality of North Wales
in the Reign of Henry Tudor', *Welsh History Review*, vol. III, no. 2,
1966.

Storey, R. L., *The End of the House of Lancaster*, Barrie & Rockliffe, 1966.

Thomas, C. H., 'The Political History of Wales from 1350–1485 as reflected in
the Literature of the period', unpublished University of Wales M.A.
dissertation, 1936. Copy available in National Library of Wales.

Thomas, R. S., 'The Political Career, Estates and "Connection" of Jasper
Tudor, Earl of Pembroke and Duke of Bedford', unpublished University
of Wales Ph.D. dissertation, 1971. Copy available in National Library
of Wales.

Vergil, Polydore, *Three Books of English History*, ed. Sir H. Ellis, Camden
Society, old series, vol. 29, 1844.

Select Bibliography

The Anglica Historia of Polydore Vergil, 1485–1537, ed. D. Hay, Camden Society, new series, vol. 74, 1950.

Walker, R. F., 'Jasper Tudor and the Town of Tenby', *National Library of Wales Journal,* vol. 16, no. 1, 1969.

Williams, D. T., *The Battle of Bosworth,* Leicester University Press, 1973.

Williams, Glanmor, *The Welsh Church from Conquest to Reformation,* University of Wales Press, 1976 edn.

Owen Glendower, Oxford University Press, 1966.

'Prophecy, Politics and Poetry in Medieval and Tudor Wales', in H. Hearder and H. R. Loyn (eds.), *British Government and Administration: Essays Presented to S. B. Chrimes,* University of Wales Press, 1974.

Williams, J. E. Caerwen, 'Twf Cenedlaethholdeb yng Nghymru'r Oesodd Canol' (Welsh national feeling in the Middle Ages), in *Gwinllan a Roddwyd,* ed. Dewi Eirug Davies, 1972. Copy in National Library of Wales.

Williams, Penry, *The Council in the Marches of Wales,* University of Wales Press, 1958.

Williams, W. Tom, 'Henry of Richmond's Itinerary to Bosworth', *Y. Cymmrodor,* vol. 29, 1919.

Wynn, John, *History of the Gwydir Family,* ed. E. T. Ballinger, University of Wales Press, 1927.

Author's Note to the Second Impression

Since the first publication of *The Son of Prophecy* in 1985 a number of studies have appeared on the period covered by this book. The subjects include the great rebellion of Owain Glyn Dwr, the central place of Wales and its poets in the civil wars of the fifteenth century, and the coming and consolidation of the Tudor dynasty. This reflects the continuing interest in a period which was to prove of great significance in the history of both Wales and England. In particular, any assessment of the Wars of the Roses must include an account of events in Wales. Accordingly I have added a number of these new works to the original Bibliography.

Two books by Professor Glanmor Williams add significantly to our understanding on the fifteenth and sixteenth centuries in Wales. *Henri Tudur a Chymru, Henry Tudor and Wales* (University of Wales Press, 1985) is a valuable addition to the St. David's Day bilingual series. In this concise study Glanmor Williams explains how the Welsh prophetic tradition and the tensions of fifteenth century society in Wales contributed to Henry's victory at Bosworth Field. The study ends with an useful survey of changing Welsh perceptions of Henry VII from Bosworth to the present.

Professor Williams's *Recovery, Reorientation and Reformation: Wales c. 1415-1642* (Oxford University Press/UWP, 1987) is already acknowledged as a classic study, described by the *Welsh History Review* as 'a major work of historical literature'. Published in the *History of Wales* series the great theme of the book is the gradual transformation of Wales from the unrest of the Glyn Dŵr era to the more settled and sure society that gradually emerged under the Tudors. Religious, social and constitutional changes are all described with equal authority.

Complementary to the themes analysed by Glanmor Williams is R. R. Davies, *The Revolt of Owain Glyn Dŵr* (OUP, 1995). Based on impressive archival documentation Professor Davies's book traces in detail the background, the development and the eventual collapse of the rising. The treatment throughout is objective in that the book demonstrates that many Welshmen preferred not to side with Glyn Dŵr. There can be little doubt that this account of the historic rebellion that transformed Wales will stand with J. E. Lloyd's *Owen Glendower* (1931).

A lively, dependable and well-illustrated account of the coming of the Tudors is Ralph A. Griffiths and Roger S. Thomas, *The Making of the Tudor Dynasty* (Alan Sutton, 1985). The book contains a full account of the complicated origins of the Royal Tudors in north Wales and the way in which Henry Tudor became involved in the fifteenth century dynastic conflict. Particularly welcome is the full treatment of Henry's years of exile in Brittany and France and the reasons why the French Crown backed the Tudor expedition of 1485.

Ralph A. Griffiths has also written a revealing, fully documented account of Henry Tudor's chief Welsh ally in *Sir Rhys ap Thomas and his Family: A Study in the Wars of the Roses and Early Tudor Politics* (UWP, 1993). Professor Griffiths notes that Sir Rhys's family was one of a small number of indigenous Welsh families which 'helped to determine the course of the Wars of the Roses by their attitudes and allegiances.' This book also includes a new, annotated edition of seventeenth century family history, 'The Life of Sir Rhys ap Thomas' (see Bibliography above).

In 1915 the late H. T. Evans (d.1950) published a classic study of *Wales and the Wars of the Roses*. The book synthesised the poetic, political and military sources on the conflict into a striking narrative which has been quoted ever since by most writers on the period. H. T. Evans's masterpiece has long been out of print but is now happily republished in a reset and illustrated edition (Alan Sutton, 1995). Introduction by Ralph A. Griffiths.

A noteworthy addition to these new studies is a fine, scholarly biography of Henry Tudor's mother by Michael K. Jones and Malcolm G. Underwood, *The King's Mother: Lady Margaret Beaufort, Countess of Richmond and Derby* (Cambridge University Press 1992). Lady Margaret was a great heiress, known for her piety, and also a descendant of John of Gaunt. It was this royal blood which inspired Henry Tudor's claim to the throne. There are a number of interesting details here of Henry's unusual upbringing with the Herberts of Raglan and (later) on his close relationship with a mother who had helped to engineer his successful bid for the throne in 1485. Much information also on Beaufort genealogy and heraldry.

A study by P. A. Johnson of *Duke Richard of York 1411-1460* (OUP, 1988) helps to show us why Wales and the Marches were central to the Yorkist strategy during the Wars of the Roses. The Yorkist leader's Mortimer lordships extended along the borders from Denbigh to

Caerleon, Ludlow was York's headquarters, and the preferred Yorkist recruiting ground lay in the Middle Marches. York was routed at Ludford Bridge in 1459 and killed the following year. But these factors were all relevant to the victory won by York's son at Mortimer's Cross in 1461, a victory which effectively gave him the throne as Edward IV.

Michael Bennett, *Lambert Simnel and the Battle of Stoke* (Alan Sutton, 1987) tells us as much as the present records allow of this little-known and hard-fought encounter in 1487. This fine piece of political and military analysis also informs us about the mysterious Yorkist conspiracies and the Irish connection behind the Stoke campaign. But the King's military deployments were decisive and victory at Stoke, sometimes known as the last battle of the Wars of the Roses, confirmed and cemented Henry VII's somewhat precarious hold on the throne after Bosworth.

The importance of the Welsh bards and seers in Henry Tudor's campaign for the throne is generally recognised. An effective and up-to-date account of this phenomenon is found in Gruffydd Aled Williams, 'The Bardic Road to Bosworth: A Welsh View of Henry Tudor' (Transactions of the Honourable Society of Cymmrodorion, 1986, pp. 7-31). This paper draws on many Welsh poetic sources and is politically shrewd in describing the appeal of vaticination and the political prophecy in fifteenth century Wales. The net result of this account is that it adds to our understanding of 'the cultural and historical imperatives' which beckoned the bards 'so irresistibly along the road to Bosworth.'

Finally, David Rees, *Sir Rhys ap Thomas* (Gomer Press, 1992) examines the career of Henry Tudor's warrior ally with special reference to his role as a bardic patron.

Index

Index

Duke of, 85, 86, 87–9, 90, 91, 94, 114

Buckingham, Edward, 3rd Duke of, 137

Builth: castle, 94; lordship, 28, 56, 72, 137

Burgundy, 77, 138

Burgundy, Margaret of, 139

Butler, Arnold, 115, 123

Byford, Lewis, 44

Cadwaladr, 12, 13, 21, 38, 46, 98, 99; Henry's descent from, 37, 107, 146; Red Dragon of, 6, 11, 123, 135, 140, 145

Caernarfon (county), 9, 141–2

Caernarfon castle, 9, 10, 18, 56

Calais, 61

Cambridge, Richard, Earl of, 51

Cardiff, 8, 18

Cardigan, 8, 19, 36, 55–6, 123–4

Cardiganshire, 1, 8, 9, 19, 56, 67, 127

Carew castle, 112, 143

Carmarthen, 25, 58, 59, 126, 140, 147–8; castle, 10, 18, 19, 35, 55–8, 59, 67, 75; eisteddfod, 36, 104

Carmarthenshire, 1, 8, 9, 56, 67, 127

Carreg Cennen castle, 18, 35–6, 55–6, 59; siege, 69–70, 110, 111

Ceri: lordship, 56, 67, 72, 142

chamberlains, 10, 26

Chandée, Philibert de, 117

Charles VIII of France, 92, 93

charters, royal, 141–2

Chepstow castle, 8

Chirk, 141–2

Chrimes, S. B., 4, 46, 48, 71, 118–19, 137

Cilgerran: castle, 54, 75, 94, 119; lordship, 54, 69

Clarence, George, Duke of, 74, 75, 76, 77, 83, 84, 138

Clarence, Lionel, Duke of, 51, 65

Commines, Philip de, 117

Conwy castle, 9, 44

counties, royal, 9–10

Courtenay, Edward, 87, 90

Courtenay, Peter, 87, 90, 91

Croyland chronicle, 123

Cumberland, 84

Cydewain: lordship, 56, 67, 72, 142

Cynan, 99

cywydd, 101

cywydd brud, 21, 102, 103–4

Dafydd ap Gwilym, 11, 101

Dafydd ap Ieuan (of Llwyndafydd), 124

Dafydd ap Ieuan ap Einon, 107

Dafydd Llwyd ap Llewellyn (of Mathafarn), 103–4, 107–8, 109, 125

Dale, 114, 118, 119, 122, 148

David Gam, 20, 25, 31

Davies, R. R., 19–20, 44

Deheubarth, 8, 9, 15, 37, 38, 42, 112

Denbigh, 17; lordship, 56, 61, 72; charter, 141–2

Devereux, Sir Walter, see Ferrers

Devon, Humphrey Stafford, Earl of, 74

Dinefwr: castle, 8, 34–5, 56, 67; lands, 34–5, 56, 110, 111, 112; town, 34–5, 36

Dinefwr, house of, 102, 109, 110, 111, 113

Dodd, A. H., 108

Dorset, Thomas Grey, Marquis of, 87, 91

dragon symbolism, 11, 13, 20–1, 99–100; used by Henry, 6, 82, 123, 135, 140, 145, 146, 147

Dryslwyn castle, 18

Dwnn, Henry, 17

Dwnn, John, 60, 67, 75

Dwnn, Lewis, 34

Dwnns of Carmarthenshire, 20

Dwnns of Kidwelly, 74

Ednyfed ap Tudur, 42, 43

Ednyfed Fychan, 33, 38–9, 40, 111, 112

Edward I, 9; Welsh settlement, 9–12, 13, 15, 39, 40

Index

Hanmer, Margaret, 16, 22
Harlech castle, 9; captured, 18, 22;
(1468), 70, 72–3, 106, 107, 112
Hastings, William, Lord, 67, 84–5
Haverfordwest, 25, 69, 123; castle, 1,
8, 69, 75, 119; lordship, 28, 137
Hay: lordship, 28, 88
Henry II, 38
Henry III, 9
Henry IV, 28, 82; and Owain Glyn
Dŵr, 16, 17, 18, 19, 22
Henry V, 3, 22, 25, 27, 29, 45–6
Henry VI, 27–8, 29, 46, 47; Wars of
the Roses, 50, 51–2, 54, 56, 60, 61–
2; deposed, 64–5, 72; Readeption,
76–7; death, 78; greyhound, 82;
King's College Chapel, 146
Henry VII (Henry Tudor, Earl of
Richmond): descent and claim to
throne, 5–6, 37, 40, 47–8, 81–3;
childhood, 59, 70–2, 76–7; in exile,
78–80, 86–96 *passim*; support,
4–5, 10, 23, 90–3, 96–7, 113–16;
return to Wales, 1–2, 96, 117–22;
march to Bosworth, 4–5, 94, 96–7,
114, 123–5, 127–30, 148; victory,
2, 31, 131–4; accession and marriage, 82, 135, 136–7; reign, 137–
44; character, 135–6, 140; Son of
Prophecy, 5, 37–8, 98, 102–9 *passim*, 144; symbolism, 2–3, 6, 82,
101–2, 144–7
Henry VIII, 10, 108–9, 138, 146
Henry ap Thomas, 75
heraldry, 144; *see also* arms
Herbert family, 74, 81, 94, 106
Herbert, Ann (née Devereux), 71, 76
Herbert, Sir Richard, 70, 72–3, 74
Herbert, Walter, 95, 123
Herbert, William, Earl of Huntingdon, 1, 72, 80, 81, 94, 141
Herbert, William, Earl of Hunting-
don, 1, 72, 80, 81, 94, 141
Herbert, Sir William, 1st Earl of
Pembroke, 31–2, 56, 58, 59, 67, 68,
69–73, 74; Son of Prophecy, 32, 50,
73, 103–8 *passim*

Hopkin ap Rhys, 69
Hopkin ap Thomas ap Einon, 21
Howard, John, *see* Norfolk
Howell Sele, 20
Hundred Years' War, 14, 25
Hungerford, Sir Walter, 25, 46
Huntingdon, Earl of, *see* Herbert,
William
Huntington: lordship, 28, 88
Hutton, W., 131
Hywel ap Goronwy, 42
Hywel Dda, 100

indentures, 140–1
Iolo Goch, 16, 43, 44
Ireland, Irish, 21, 25, 28, 63, 138, 144

John ap Gruffydd ap Nicholas, 110
John ap Meredith, 95–6
John of Gaunt, 47, 51, 52, 81–2
Jones, E. D., 108
justice, in Wales, 28–9, 141
justiciars, 10, 26

Katherine, Queen, 46–7, 48, 60
Kidwelly, 127; castle, 36, 55–6;
lordship, 28, 35, 56
King's College, Cambridge: Chapel,
146

Lancaster, Duchy of: estates, 28, 68,
80, 82; revenues, 137
Lancaster, house of, 50–1, 56, 82,
104; united with York, 2–3, 136,
145
land-holding, in Wales, 10–11, 14,
15, 26, 142
Lander, J. R., 27
Landois, Peter, 80, 92
law, in Wales, 8, 10–11; *see also*
penal legislation
Laws, Edward, 118
Leland, John, 22, 112
Lewis, Edward, 87, 114
Lewis Glyn Cothi, 60, 73, 75, 101,
103–5, 109, 111–12, 116, 144
Lewis Mon, 142

167

Index

Index

Northumberland, Henry Percy, 4th Earl of, 91, 131, 134

official class, Welsh, 11, 15, 34, 40
officialdom, English, in Wales, 10, 15, 26, 27–8
Owain ap Gruffydd ap Nicholas, 55–6, 58, 60, 69, 70, 110
Owain (ap Urien Rheged), 12, 34, 98
Owain Glyn Dŵr, 15–16, 42; rebellion, 15, 16–22, 33, 44–5, 49, 98, 102; results, 22–5, 26, 28, 30, 34, 103
Owain Lawgoch, 13–14, 102–3
Owen, George, 118, 119, 143–4
Oxford, John de la Vere, Earl of, 93, 131, 132, 134

Parry, Sir Thomas, 99
Pembroke, 14; earldom, 47, 54, 69, 73, 80, 123; lordship, 54–5, 56, 68, 69, 80, 137, 140–1
Pembroke castle, 8, 55, 59, 68, 70–1, 76, 78, 118, 119–22
penal legislation, 5, 17, 22, 24, 25, 30, 141
Penmynydd, 42, 43, 45
Pennal Policy, 19
Pernrhyn, 33
Percy family, 30, 52
Percy, Henry (Hotspur), 18
Percy, Henry, 4th Earl of Northumberland, 91, 131, 134
Picquigny, Treaty of, 79
Pilleth, 18
Plantagenet, Katherine, 94
poetry: courtly, 11, 101; prophetic, 5, 11–13, 20–1, 37–8, 73, 96–100, 101–9. See also bards
portcullis, Beaufort, 82, 146
Powys, 105; princes of, 8, 15, 38
primogeniture, 11, 142
Prince of Wales's Council, 81, 141
Prince of Wales: native, 7; English, 11
Principality, 9–11, 14, 26–8; in Wars

of the Roses, 56, 68, 80, 81; under Henry VII, 137, 141
prophecy, see poetry, prophetic
Pwll Melyn, 19

racial tension, 12, 13–15, 22, 101, 142
Raglan: castle, 71, 78; lordship, 72
ravens, 34, 102, 109, 113, 116, 147–8
Rhodri Mawr, 21, 37, 38
Rhuddlan, Statue of, 9–10
Rhydderch ap Rhys, 55–6
Rhys, the Lord, 8, 9, 38, 112
Rhys ap Gruffydd, Sir (d. 1356), 11
Rhys ap Gruffydd, Sir (d. 1531), 109, 114
Rhys ap Maredudd, 9
Rhys ap Thomas, Sir, 36, 39, 91, 102, 111, 112–13; supports Henry, 96–7, 108, 113–16, 123, 125–6, 127; rewarded, 116, 137, 143; tomb, 147–8
Rhys ap Tudur, 33, 42, 43–4, 45
Rhys Fawr ap Meredudd, 127, 134
Rice family, 33, 114
Richard II, 16, 26, 44, 82
Richard III: as Duke of Gloucester, 75, 76, 80, 83–6; as king, 1–2, 86–96 passim, 106–7, 114, 119–22, 123, 124, 128–9; defeat and death, 4, 116, 132–4; badge, 3, 101
Richard ap Howell, 127
Richmond, 1st Earl of, see Tudor, Edmund
Richmond, 2nd Earl of, see Henry VII
Rivers, Earl, 84, 85
Robert III of Scotland, 21
Roberts, Glyn, 26, 40
'Rose of England, The', 126
roses: symbolism, 2–3, 145, 146
Ross, Charles, 65, 84, 117, 128, 131
Rotherham, Archbishop, 85
Rowse, A. L., 127
Ruthin, 17; lordship, 142
Rutland, Edmund, Earl of, 63

St Albans, battle of: first, 54, 55; second, 64

169

Index

Index